CW00550809

THE
TEST
CRICKETER'S
ALMANAC

Jason Woolgar

Eric Dobby Publishing

Published by Eric Dobby Publishing Ltd,
12 Warnford Road, Orpington, Kent BR6 6LW

A catalogue record of this book is available from
the British Library.

ISBN 1-85882-009-X

Typeset in Times by Kevin O'Connor, Poole
Printed and bound in Great Britain by
BPCC Hazell Books Ltd
Member of BPCC Ltd

**This book is dedicated to
Mum and Dad**

Elaine & Barry Woolgar

Acknowledgments

The Publishers would like to thank Patrick
Eagar, David Munden and Allsport Ltd for allowing them to reproduce their photographs in this
book.

All the photographs are with the permission of
Patrick Eagar with the exception Murphy Su'a
which is with the permission of Allsport Ltd and of
the following which are with the permission of
David Munden:–

K. Arnott, T. Blains, A. Brades, D. Brain,
A. Flower, G. Flower, D. Houghton.

Contents

Foreword

by Mike Selvey

It is fair to say that ever since Silver Billy Balham smacked the ball all over Hambledon, and Lumpy Stevens tore in over the hill, there have been arguments about the relative merits of cricketers. It is what has made cricket the most statistical of games, more figure-conscious than any super model (and even providing gainful employment for those who might otherwise get their kicks in the VAT office). Now call me a crusty old traditionalist if you like, but I was rather fond of the good old fashioned averages as a means of settling such debate. You knew precisely where you stood with them: they told you all you needed to know about a player. Bradman: 50 innings, 10 times not out, 6996 runs, average 99.94 means a hell of a batsman. No argument.

However, statistics, like the bikinis on the beaches in the Caribbean (life as a cricketing correspondent of a national newspaper does carry some perks), while made to reveal an awful lot, are also designed to conceal certain elements as well. Lies, damned lies, and batting averages, as the Iron Duke probably would have said. So just because Viv Richards had a Test match average fractionally over half that of Bradman doesn't necessarily imply that the Don was twice as good. And the same principle holds with bowlers as well.

In other words, with no account taken of circumstance, conditions, and other variables, such as the quality of the opposition, averages don't tell the truth, the whole truth and nothing but the truth. So while the argument as to whether Bradman would have made quite as many runs were he playing today has sustained many a cricket club bar into the small hours, it has been completely hypothetical.

Likewise, any attempt to compare the merits of contemporary players. And then along *came the* Deloittes, now Coopers & Lybrand, ratings. Now these were not designed to take the place of the averages because there is no attempt to quantify performance in terms of runs, or wickets. Instead, they could be regarded as supplementary, and taking into account such variables as previously mentioned, international players can now be allocated a position in a peer group. It's not a new concept. Golfers, for example, have been ranked for years but with the complexities of cricket, it required the computer age and a fertile mind to the bring the idea to fruition. Thus any argument concerning who is the best batsman in the world now can be prefaced immediately with the words "well, according to Coopers and Lybrand ..." It's a smarter sort of reply, kills the debate stone dead and won't swell the bar profits, but probably as near accurate an assessment as can be. The ratings are certainly here to stay, even for this curmudgeon.

INTRODUCTION

Forced to compete with the media and sponsors' demands for faster, less time consuming sports, Test cricket has undergone major changes within the last few years. Given a new impetus by the re-emergence of South Africa, and the introduction of Zimbabwe as the ninth Test-playing nation, growing numbers of spectators have witnessed over fifty Test matches in the last fifteen months alone. Rule changes, coupled with neutral umpires and the use of television replays, have coincided with more positive attitudes. Attitudes further enhanced by the introduction of exciting new talent and a refreshing variation in approach.

The past year has seen an increased number of matches with no one team completely dominating the Test scene. Although the West Indies remain unbeaten, the once huge gap in class has narrowed, a fact highlighted recently when Australia pushed them to within 2 runs of a first series defeat since 1979-80. Trailing 1-0 with two Test matches to play, the West Indies seemed poised to level the series when Australia, needing 186 to clinch victory, slumped to 74-7. However 110 runs added by the next 2 wickets took Australia to within 2 runs of victory when the final twist saw Craig McDermott caught behind off Courtney Walsh to give the West Indies a breathtaking win by just one run. With the rubber level and Australia in disarray, the West Indies went on to clinch the series in convincing style in the next Test. Despite this setback, Australia bounced back to inflict another crushing Ashes defeat on England in 1993. In the process Allan Border broke Donald Bradman's captaincy record of unbeaten matches against England, leading them 18 times in succession before finally losing the last Test at the Oval. This record is just one of a host to fall to Border. He is the first ever batsman to score 11000 Test runs and has played more matches, taken more catches, and passed fifty on more occasions than any other player in Test match history. Australia have in Merv Hughes and Craig McDermott two of the best fast bowlers in world cricket, both of whom have taken over two hundred Test wickets. These two are superbly complemented by the deadly leg-spinner Shane Warne, who has already taken over 100 wickets in his short Test career. Also a strong batting side, David Boon and Mark Taylor are two of cricket's heaviest accumulators of runs, and the twins Steve and Mark Waugh are both attacking, stylish batsmen. However, an inability to successfully chase moderate last innings totals has seen them lose Test matches well within their grasp, the latest of which came in the drawn home series against South Africa.

South Africa have already proved themselves to be of the highest calibre since their reintroduction to Test cricket, losing just one of ten matches following their comeback defeat against the West Indies in 1992. They have since enjoyed victories against Sri Lanka and India and drew a tough rubber in Australia. They have many quality players, particularly Allan Donald, a genuine fast bowler who has already taken 51 Test wickets in just 11 matches.

Although Zimbabwe have not yet managed a Test win, their early performances have been encouraging. Their 1992 draw against India was the best inaugural Test match result of any nation since Australia beat England in the very first Test of 1887. Despite subsequent defeats by India and New Zealand they recently pushed Pakistan closer than a 2-0 defeat would suggest. Often promisingly placed, inexperience has cost them dearly at key moments. Needing to occupy the crease for just 69 overs to draw the First Test, they were bowled out for 134. In the Second they were excellently placed at 131-1 needing 240 to level the series, but they again collapsed, losing their last 9 wickets for just 52 runs.

In fact it is the ability of the Pakistani pace duo Wasim Akram and Waqar Younis to consistently defend low totals that has made Pakistan one of the most dangerous sides in Test cricket. Wasim Akram recently became the 29th bowler to take over 200 Test wickets and his current total stands at 222 in 53 matches. Waqar Younis' record is even more impressive having taken an incredible 166 wickets in just 29 Test matches. He is currently the world's best bowler, a fact reiterated by an amazing strike rate averaging a wicket every six overs. Also a gifted batting side, Pakistan have lost just two Test series in the last nine years. Their most accomplished batsman Javed Miandad is the third highest scorer in Test cricket, having registered almost 9000 runs.

Two of the other Test-playing nations, New Zealand and Sri Lanka, are currently going through transitional periods and are both struggling as a result.

New Zealand, still attempting to replace established players, have been further hampered by an injury to influential skipper Martin Crowe. They have won just one Test series, against Zimbabwe, since they defeated India in 1990, and recently lost four successive matches against Australia and Pakistan. New players have constantly failed to provide adequate support for the top order batsmen Martin Crowe and Andrew Jones, and Danny Morrison is often isolated as their one quality bowler. They have, however, enough young promising players to suggest that given further opportunities they could develop into a good side. Encouragingly enough, they ended their recent dismal run with an excellent five wicket win in the Third Test against Pakistan.

Sri Lanka, despite successive victories against New Zealand and England in 92/93, have failed to win again in their next ten attempts. However, top batsmen Aravinda De Silva and captain Arjuna Ranatunga have still managed to score over 2500 Test runs each. Their spinner 21-year-old Muttiah Muralitharan is an outstanding prospect, having already taken 52 wickets in just 13 matches. He was the one bowler able to trouble the Indian batsmen in the recent Test series in which Sri Lanka were crushed 3-0.

This victory was the second whitewash inflicted by an outstanding Indian team in the last 15 months, having already defeated England 3-0 in the 92/93 series. Their batting line-up is one of the strongest in the world and they have in Sachin Tendulkar and Vinod Kambli two of cricket's major young talents. Tendulkar, India's youngest ever Test player at 16 years 205 days, has already scored almost 2000 Test runs and is one of the few batsmen to maintain an average of over 50. Kambli's entrance to the Test arena has been exceptional, with almost 1000 runs in just ten matches. At one stage he made successive scores of 224, 227, 125, 4, and 120 and already averages an incredible 93.70. When you include Mohammad Azharuddin in this batting order it is easy to see how India have won 7 of their last 10 Test matches. A varied bowling attack includes leg-spinner Anil Kumble, and the all-rounder Kapil Dev, who surpassed Richard Hadlee's world record total of 431 Test wickets in the recent series against Sri Lanka. One of the game's greats, Kapil Dev is the only player to score 5000 runs and take 400 wickets in Test match history.

The lack of an all-rounder, or more significantly a replacement for Ian Botham, has been one of the factors in England's consistent failure at the highest level. Without a series victory since they defeated New Zealand in February 1992, England have won just two of their previous 15 Tests. In the process they suffered the humiliation of a first ever defeat against Sri Lanka, a 3-0 whitewash by India and another Ashes debacle against Australia. An unreliable selection policy has precipitated this disastrous sequence of results, with some 36 players used in just 15 matches, many being discarded after a handful of appearances. The decisions to continuously omit David Gower and to persevere with Alex Stewart as wicket-keeper have proved to be both misguided and ineffective. Despite a batting line-up talented enough to take on any attack, England are still prone to collapse and their bowling with few exceptions has been moderate. However they have some excellent players and with a more consistent selection strategy could produce a team capable of beating any Test side. They gave notice of their potential in the last Test match against Australia at the Oval in 1993, winning by 161 runs in Michael Atherton's second match as captain.

If the English revival is to continue this winter they will have to overcome a formidable West Indian team, who convincingly defeated Pakistan 2-0 in their recent series. Captain Ritchie Richardson is an outstanding batsmen and Desmond Haynes returned to form against Pakistan scoring 402 runs in 3 completed innings at an average of 134. Curtley Ambrose and Courtney Walsh are still two of the fastest and most aggressive bowlers in the world and Brian Lara looks certain to continue the attacking tradition of West Indian batsmen as his 277 against Australia testifies.

With so much cricket now being played, this book aims to reflect the constant changes in the Test game, updating the major records, introducing exciting new players and reviewing the careers of those already established. Although the cricketers included are a personal choice, the majority demanded selection having enjoyed great success at the highest level. However, for the sake of parity I have included some players from the weaker nations who have not yet altogether excelled

The statistical profiles on each cricketer represent their Test careers only and are complete up to and including the New Zealand versus Pakistan series which finished in March 1994.

Finally I would like to take this opportunity to thank Coopers and Lybrand for allowing their ratings to be used in a book for the first time, with special thanks to Gordon Vince who kindly supplied the ranking tables, including each player's particular rating.

Jason Woolgar

TEST MATCH RESULTS
OCT 92 - FEB 94

Zimbabwe v India   Oct 92
Only Test Harare   Match drawn

Zimbabwe v New Zealand   Oct 92 - Nov 92
1st Test   Bulawayo   Match drawn
2nd Test   Harare   New Zealand won by 177 runs

South Africa v India   Nov 92 - Jan 93
1st Test   Durban   Match drawn
2nd Test   Johannesburg Match drawn
3rd Test   Port Elizabeth South Africa won by 9
                        wickets
4th Test   Cape Town   Match drawn

Australia v West Indies   Nov 92 - Feb 93
1st Test   Brisbane   Match drawn
2nd Test   Melbourne   Australia won by 139 runs
3rd Test   Sydney   Match drawn
4th Test   Adelaide   West Indies won by 1 run
5th Test   Perth   West Indies won by an innings
                        and 25 runs

Sri Lanka v New Zealand   Nov 92 - Dec 92
1st Test   Moratuwa   Match drawn
2nd Test   Colombo   Sri Lanka won by 9 wickets

New Zealand v Pakistan   Jan 93
Only Test Hamilton   Pakistan won by 33 runs

India v England   Jan 93 - Feb 93
1st Test   Calcutta   India won by 8 wickets
2nd Test   Madras   India won by an innings and 22
                        runs
3rd Test   Bombay   India won by an innings and 15
                        runs

New Zealand v Australia   Feb 93 - Mar 93
1st Test   Christchurch Australia won by an innings
                        and 60 runs
2nd Test   Wellington   Match drawn
3rd Test   Auckland   New Zealand won by 5 wickets

Sri Lanka v England   Mar 93
Only Test Colombo   Sri Lanka won by 5 wickets

India v Zimbabwe   Mar 93
Only Test Delhi   India won by an innings and 13
                        runs

West Indies v Pakistan   Apr 93 - May 93
1st Test   Port of Spain West Indies won by 204
                        runs
2nd Test   Bridgetown   West Indies won by 10 wickets
3rd Test   St John's   Match drawn

England v Australia   June 93 - Aug 93
1st Test   Old Trafford Australia won by 179 runs
2nd Test   Lord's   Australia won by an innings and 62 runs
3rd Test   Trent Bridge Match drawn
4th Test   Headingley   Australia won by an innings and 148 runs
5th Test   Edgbaston   Australia won by 8 wickets
6th Test   The Oval   England won by 161 runs

Sri Lanka v India   July 93 - Aug 93
1st Test   Kandy   Match drawn
2nd Test   Colombo   India won by 235 runs
3rd Test   Colombo   Match drawn

Sri Lanka v South Africa   Aug 93 - Sept 93
1st Test   Moratuwa   Match drawn
2nd Test   Colombo   South Africa won by an innings and 208 runs
3rd Test   Colombo   Match drawn

Australia v New Zealand   Nov 93 - Dec 93
1st Test   Perth   Match drawn
2nd Test   Hobart   Australia won by an innings and 222 runs
3rd Test   Brisbane   Australia won by an innings and 96 runs

Pakistan v Zimbabwe   Dec 93
1st Test   Karachi   Pakistan won by 131 runs
2nd Test   Rawalpindi   Pakistan won by 52 runs
3rd Test   Lahore   Match drawn

Sri Lanka v West Indies   Dec 93
Only Test Moratuwa   Match drawn

Australia v South Africa   Dec 93 - Feb 94
1st Test   Melbourne   Match drawn
2nd Test   Sydney   South Africa won by 5 runs
3rd Test   Adelaide   Australia won by 191 runs

India v Sri Lanka   Jan 94 - Feb 94
1st Test   Lucknow   India won by an innings and 119 runs
2nd Test   Bangalore   India won by an innings and 95 runs
3rd Test   Ahmedabad   India won by an innings and 17 runs

New Zealand v Pakistan   Feb 94
1st Test   Auckland   Pakistan won by 5 wickets
2nd Test   Wellington   Pakistan won by an innings and 12 runs
3rd Test   Christchurch New Zealand won by 5 wickets

TEST MATCH RESULTS

AUSTRALIA

Opposition	First Match	Tests	Won	Drawn	Lost	Tied
England	1877	280	108	83	89	0
India	1947	50	24	17	8	1
New Zealand	1946	32	13	12	7	0
Pakistan	1956	34	12	13	9	0
South Africa	1902	56	30	14	12	0
Sri Lanka	1983	7	4	3	0	0
West Indies	1930	77	30	20	26	1
Total		536	221	162	151	2

ENGLAND

Opposition	First Match	Tests	Won	Drawn	Lost	Tied
Australia	1877	280	89	83	108	0
India	1932	81	31	36	14	0
New Zealand	1930	72	33	35	4	0
Pakistan	1954	52	14	31	7	0
South Africa	1889	102	46	38	18	0
Sri Lanka	1982	5	3	1	1	0
West Indies	1928	104	24	37	43	0
Total		696	240	261	195	0

INDIA

Opposition	First Match	Tests	Won	Drawn	Lost	Tied
Australia	1947	50	8	17	24	1
England	1932	81	14	36	31	0
New Zealand	1955	31	12	13	6	0
Pakistan	1952	44	4	33	7	0
South Africa	1992	4	0	3	1	0
Sri Lanka	1982	14	7	6	1	0
West Indies	1948	62	6	30	26	0
Zimbabwe	1992	2	1	1	0	0
Total		288	52	139	96	1

NEW ZEALAND

Opposition	First Match	Tests	Won	Drawn	Lost	Tied
Australia	1946	32	7	12	13	0
England	1930	72	4	35	33	0
India	1955	31	6	13	12	0
Pakistan	1955	36	4	16	16	0
South Africa	1932	17	2	6	9	0
Sri Lanka	1983	11	4	6	1	0
West Indies	1952	24	4	12	8	0
Zimbabwe	1992	2	1	1	0	0
Total		225	32	101	92	0

PAKISTAN

Opposition	First Match	Tests	Won	Drawn	Lost	Tied
Australia	1956	34	9	13	12	0
England	1954	52	7	31	14	0
India	1952	44	7	33	4	0
New Zealand	1955	36	16	16	4	0
Sri Lanka	1982	12	6	5	1	0
West Indies	1958	31	7	12	12	0
Zimbabwe	1993	3	2	1	0	0
Total		212	54	111	47	0

SOUTH AFRICA

Opposition	First Match	Tests	Won	Drawn	Lost	Tied
Australia	1902	56	12	14	30	0
England	1889	102	18	38	46	0
India	1992	4	1	3	0	0
New Zealand	1932	17	9	6	2	0
Sri Lanka	1993	3	1	2	0	0
West Indies	1992	1	0	0	1	0
Total		183	41	63	79	0

SRI LANKA

Opposition	First Match	Tests	Won	Drawn	Lost	Tied
Australia	1983	7	0	3	4	0
England	1982	5	1	1	3	0
India	1982	14	1	6	7	0
New Zealand	1983	11	1	6	4	0
Pakistan	1982	12	1	5	6	0
South Africa	1993	3	0	2	1	0
West Indies	1993	1	0	1	0	0
Total		53	4	24	25	0

WEST INDIES

Opposition	First Match	Tests	Won	Drawn	Lost	Tied
Australia	1930	77	26	20	30	1
England	1928	104	43	37	24	0
India	1948	62	26	30	6	0
New Zealand	1952	24	8	12	4	0
Pakistan	1958	31	12	12	7	0
South Africa	1992	1	1	0	0	0
Sri Lanka	1993	1	0	1	0	0
Total		300	116	112	71	1

ZIMBABWE

Opposition	First Match	Tests	Won	Drawn	Lost	Tied
India	1992	2	0	1	1	0
New Zealand	1992	2	0	1	1	0
Pakistan	1993	3	0	1	2	0
Total		7	0	3	4	0

TOTAL TEST MATCH RESULTS

	Tests	Won	Drawn	Lost	Tied
Australia	536	221	162	151	2
England	696	240	261	195	0
India	288	52	139	96	1
New Zealand	225	32	101	92	0
Pakistan	212	54	111	47	0
South Africa	183	41	63	79	0
Sri Lanka	53	4	24	25	0
West Indies	300	116	112	71	1
Zimbabwe	7	0	3	4	0

HIGHEST TEST INNINGS

903 for 7 dec	England v Australia	The Oval	1938
849	England v West Indies	Kingston	1929-30
790	West Indies v Pakistan	Kingston	1957-58
758 for 8 dec	Australia v West Indies	Kingston	1954-55
729 for 6 dec	Australia v England	Lord's	1930
708	Pakistan v England	The Oval	1987
701	Australia v England	The Oval	1934
699 for 5 dec	Pakistan v India	Lahore	1989-90
695	Australia v England	The Oval	1930
687 for 8 dec	West Indies v England	The Oval	1976
681 for 8 dec	West Indies v England	Port of Spain	1953-54
676 for 7 dec	India v Sri Lanka	Kanpur	1986-87
674	Australia v India	Adelaide	1947-48
674	Pakistan v India	Faisalabad	1984-85
671 for 7 dec	New Zealand v Sri Lanka	Wellington	1990-91
668	Australia v West Indies	Bridgetown	1954-55
659 for 8 dec	Australia v England	Sydney	1946-47
658 for 8 dec	England v Australia	Trent Bridge	1938
657 for 8 dec	Pakistan v West Indies	Bridgetown	1957-58
656 for 8 dec	Australia v England	Old Trafford	1964
654 for 5	England v South Africa	Durban	1938-39
653 for 4 dec	England v India	Lord's	1990
653 for 4 dec	Australia v England	Headingley	1993
652 for 8 dec	West Indies v England	Lord's	1973
652	Pakistan v India	Faisalabad	1982-83
652 for 7 dec	England v India	Madras	1984 85
650 for 6 dec	Australia v West Indies	Bridgetown	1964-65

LOWEST COMPLETED TEST INNINGS

26	New Zealand v England	Auckland	1954-55
30	South Africa v England	Port Elizabeth	1895-96
30	South Africa v England	Edgbaston	1924
35	South Africa v England	Cape Town	1898-99
36	Australia v England	Edgbaston	1902
36	South Africa v Australia	Melbourne	1931-32
42	Australia v England	Sydney	1887-88
42	New Zealand v Australia	Wellington	1945-46
42[1]	India v England	Lord's	1974
43	South Africa v England	Cape Town	1888-89
44	Australia v England	The Oval	1896
45	England v Australia	Sydney	1886-87
45	South Africa v Australia	Melbourne	1931-32
47	South Africa v England	Cape Town	1888-89
47	New Zealand v England	Lord's	1958
52	England v Australia	The Oval	1948
53	England v Australia	Lord's	1888
53	Australia v England	Lord's	1896
53	West Indies v Pakistan	Faisalabad	1986-87
54	New Zealand v Australia	Wellington	1945-46
58	South Africa v England	Lord's	1912
58[2]	Australia v England	Brisbane	1936-37
58	India v Australia	Brisbane	1947-48
58	India v England	Old Trafford	1952
60	Australia v England	Lord's	1888
61	Australia v England	Melbourne	1901-02
61	England v Australia	Melbourne	1903-04
62	England v Australia	Lord's	1888
62	Pakistan v Australia	Perth	1981-82
63	Australia v England	The Oval	1882
64	England v New Zealand	Wellington	1977-78
65	England v Australia	Sydney	1894-95
65	Australia v England	The Oval	1912
65	New Zealand v England	Christchurch	1970-71

[1] One batsman absent hurt
[2] One batsman absent ill

GREATEST TEST MATCH VICTORIES

Inns and 579 runs	England v Australia	The Oval	1938
Inns and 336 runs	West Indies v India	Calcutta	1958-59
Inns and 332 runs	Australia v England	Brisbane	1946-47
Inns and 285 runs	England v India	Lord's	1974
Inns and 259 runs	Australia v South Africa	Port Elizabeth	1949-50
Inns and 237 runs	England v West Indies	The Oval	1957
Inns and 230 runs	England v Australia	Adelaide	1891-92
Inns and 226 runs	Australia v India	Brisbane	1947-48
Inns and 226 runs	West Indies v England	Lord's	1973
Inns and 225 runs	England v Australia	Melbourne	1911-12
Inns and 222 runs	Australia v New Zealand	Hobart	1993-94
Inns and 217 runs	England v Australia	The Oval	1886
Inns and 217 runs	Australia v West Indies	Brisbane	1930-31
Inns and 215 runs	England v New Zealand	Auckland	1962-63
Inns and 208 runs	South Africa v Sri Lanka	Colombo	1993-94
Inns and 207 runs	England v India	Old Trafford	1952
Inns and 202 runs	England v South Africa	Cape Town	1888-89
Inns and 200 runs	Australia v England	Melbourne	1936-37
675 runs	England v Australia	Brisbane	1928-29
562 runs	Australia v England	The Oval	1934
530 runs	Australia v South Africa	Melbourne	1910-11
425 runs	West Indies v England	Old Trafford	1976
409 runs	Australia v England	Lord's	1948
408 runs	West Indies v Australia	Adelaide	1979-80
382 runs	Australia v England	Adelaide	1894-95
382 runs	Australia v West Indies	Sydney	1968-69
377 runs	Australia v England	Sydney	1920-21
365 runs	Australia v England	Melbourne	1936-37
348 runs	Australia v Pakistan	Melbourne	1976-77
343 runs	West Indies v Australia	Bridgetown	1990-91
338 runs	England v Australia	Adelaide	1932-33
326 runs	West Indies v England	Lord's	1950
323 runs	South Africa v Australia	Port Elizabeth	1969-70
322 runs	England v Australia	Brisbane	1936-37
312 runs	England v South Africa	Cape Town	1956-57
308 runs	Australia v England	Melbourne	1907-08
307 runs	Australia v England	Sydney	1924-25
307 runs	South Africa v Australia	Johannesburg	1969-70
300 runs	Australia v India	Perth	1991-92

NARROWEST TEST MATCH VICTORIES

One wicket victories

			10th Wkt
England v Australia	The Oval	1902	15*
South Africa v England	Johannesburg	1905-06	48*
England v Australia	Melbourne	1907-08	39*
England v South Africa	Cape Town	1922-23	5*
Australia v West Indies	Melbourne	1951-52	38*
New Zealand v West Indies	Dunedin	1979-80	4*

Two wicket victories

			9th Wkt
England v Australia	The Oval	1890	2*
Australia v England	Sydney	1907-08	56*
England v South Africa[1]	Durban	1948-49	12*
Australia v West Indies	Melbourne	1960-61	2*
India v Australia	Bombay	1964-65	32*
Australia v India	Perth	1977-78	12*
West Indies v England	Trent Bridge	1980	4*
New Zealand v Pakistan	Dunedin	1984-85	50*
West Indies v Pakistan	Bridgetown	1987-88	61*
Pakistan v England	Lord's	1992	46*

England won with a leg bye off the last ball

Victories by less than 20 runs

Runs			
1	West Indies v Australia	Adelaide	1992-93
3	Australia v England	Old Trafford	1902
3	England v Australia	Melbourne	1982-83
5	South Africa v Australia	Sydney	1993-94
6	Australia v England	Sydney	1884-85
7	Australia v England	The Oval	1882
10	England v Australia	Sydney	1894-95
11	Australia v England	Adelaide	1924-25
12	England v Australia	Adelaide	1928-29
13	England v Australia	Sydney	1886-87
16	Australia v India	Brisbane	1977-78
16	Pakistan v India	Bangalore	1986-87
16	Australia v Sri Lanka	Colombo	1992-93
17	South Africa v England	Johannesburg	1956-57
18	England v Australia	Headingley	1981
19	South Africa v England	Johannesburg	1909-10

TIED TEST MATCHES

Australia v West Indies	Brisbane	1960-61
India v Australia	Madras	1986-87

MOST APPEARANCES IN TEST MATCH CRICKET

Player	Team	Tests	Opposition								
			Aus	Eng	Ind	NZ	Pak	SA	SL	WI	Zim
A.R. Border	Aus	153	-	47	20	23	22	3	7	31	0
Kapil Dev	Ind	130	20	27	-	9	29	4	14	25	2
S.M. Gavaskar	Ind	125	20	33	-	9	24	0	7	27	0
Javed Miandad	Pak	124	24	22	28	18	-	0	12	17	3
I.V.A. Richards	WI	121	34	36	28	7	16	0	0	-	0
D.I. Gower	Eng	117	42	-	24	13	17	0	2	19	0
D.B. Vengsarkar	Eng	116	24	26	-	11	22	0	8	25	0
M.C. Cowdrey	Eng	114	43	-	8	18	10	14	0	21	0
D.L. Haynes	WI	112	33	32	19	10	15	1	1	-	0
C.H. Lloyd	WI	110	29	34	28	8	11	0	0	-	0
J. Boycott	Eng	108	38	-	13	15	5	7	0	29	0
C.G. Greenidge	WI	108	29	32	23	10	14	0	0	-	0
G.A. Gooch	Eng	107	37	-	19	12	13	0	3	26	0
I.T. Botham	Eng	102	36	-	14	15	14	0	3	20	0

LEADING TEST MATCH RUN SCORERS

Name	Team	Mat	Inns	NO	Runs	HS	Avg	100	50
A.R. Border	Aus	153	260	43	11022	205	50.79	27	63
S.M. Gavaskar	Ind	125	214	16	10122	236 *	51.12	34	45
Javed Miandad	Pak	124	189	21	8832	280 *	52.57	23	43
I.V.A. Richards	WI	121	182	12	8540	291	50.23	24	45
G.A. Gooch	Eng	107	195	6	8293	333	43.87	19	45
D.I. Gower	Eng	117	204	18	8231	215	44.25	18	39
G. Boycott	Eng	108	193	23	8114	246 *	47.72	22	42
G.S. Sobers	WI	93	160	21	8032	365 *	57.78	26	30
M.C. Cowdrey	Eng	114	188	15	7624	182	44.06	22	38
C.G. Greenidge	WI	108	185	16	7558	226	44.72	19	34
C.H. Lloyd	WI	110	175	14	7515	242 *	46.67	19	39
D.L. Haynes	WI	112	195	24	7270	184	42.51	18	38
W.R. Hammond	Eng	85	140	16	7249	336 *	58.45	22	24
G.S. Chappell	Aus	87	151	19	7110	247 *	53.86	24	31
D.B. Bradman	Aus	52	80	10	6996	334	99.94	29	13
L. Hutton	Eng	79	138	15	6971	364	56.67	19	33
D.B. Vengsarkar	Ind	116	185	22	6868	166	42.13	17	35
K.F. Barrington	Eng	82	131	15	6806	256	58.67	20	35
D.C. Boon	Aus	86	154	17	6287	200	45.89	18	28
R.B. Kanhai	WI	79	137	6	6227	256	47.53	15	28
R.N. Harvey	Aus	79	137	10	6149	205	48.41	21	24
G.R. Viswanath	Ind	91	155	10	6080	222	41.93	14	35

HIGHEST INDIVIDUAL TEST SCORES

375	B.C. Lara	West Indies v England	St John's	1993-94
365*	G.S. Sobers	West Indies v Pakistan	Kingston	1957-58
364	L. Hutton	England v Australia	The Oval	1938
337	Hanif Mohammad	Pakistan v West Indies	Bridgetown	1957-58
336*	W.R. Hammond	England v New Zealand	Auckland	1932-33
334	D.G. Bradman	Australia v England	Headingley	1930
333	G.A. Gooch	England v India	Lord's	1990
325	A. Sandham	England v West Indies	Kingston	1929-30
311	R.B. Simpson	Australia v England	Old Trafford	1964
310	J.H. Edrich	England v New Zealand	Headingley	1965
307	R.M. Cowper	Australia v England	Melbourne	1965-66
304	D.G. Bradman	Australia v South Africa	Adelaide	1931-32
302	L.G. Rowe	West Indies v England	Bridgetown	1973-74
299*	D.G. Bradman	Australia v South Africa	Adelaide	1931-32
299	M.D. Crowe	New Zealand v Sri Lanka	Wellington	1990-91
291	I.V.A. Richards	West Indies v England	The Oval	1976
287	R.E. Foster	England v Australia	Sydney	1903-04
285*	P.B.H. May	England v West Indies	Birmingham	1958
280*	Javed Miandad	Pakistan v India	Hyderabad	1982-83
278	D.C.S. Compton	England v Pakistan	Trent Bridge	1954
277	B.C. Lara	West Indies v Australia	Sydney	1992-93
274	R.G. Pollock	South Africa v Australia	Durban	1969-70
274	Zaheer Abbas	Pakistan v England	Edgbaston	1971
271	Javed Miandad	Pakistan v New Zealand	Auckland	1988-89
270*	G.A. Headley	West Indies v England	Kingston	1934-35
270	D.G. Bradman	Australia v England	Melbourne	1936-37

HIGHEST TEST PARTNERSHIPS
FOR EACH WICKET

Wkt	Runs	Teams	Venue	Year	Batsmen
1st	413	Ind v NZ	Madras	1955-56	M.H. Mankad/ Pankaj Roy
2nd	451	Aus v Eng	The Oval	1934	W.H. Ponsford/ D.G. Bradburn
3rd	467	NZ v SL	Wellington	1990-91	A.H. Jones/ M. D. Crowe
4th	411	Eng v WI	Birmingham	1957	P.B.H. May/ M. C. Cowdrey
5th	405	Aus v Eng	Sydney	1946-47	S.G. Barnes/ D. G. Bradman
6th	346	Aus v Eng	Melbourne	1936-37	J.H.W. Fingleton/ D.G. Bradman
7th	347	WI v Aus	Bridgetown	1954-55	D.S. Atkinson/ C. C. Depeiza
8th	246	Eng v NZ	Lord's	1931	L.E.G. Ames/ G.O.B. Allen
9th	190	Pak v Eng	The Oval	1967	Asif Iqbal/ Intikhab Alam
10th	151	NZ v Pak	Auckland	1972-73	B.F Hastings/ R.O. Collinge

TOTAL HIGHEST TEST PARTNERSHIPS

Runs	Wkt	Teams	Venue	Year	Batsmen
467	3rd	NZ v SL	Wellington	1990-91	A.H. Jones/ M. D. Crowe
451	2nd	Aus v Eng	The Oval	1938	W.H. Ponsford/ D.G. Bradman
451	3rd	Pak v Ind	Hyderabad	1982-83	Mudassar Nazar/ Javed Miandad
446	2nd	WI v Pak	Kingston	1957-58	C.C. Hunte/ G.S. Sobers
413	1st	Ind v NZ	Madras	1955-56	M.H. Mankad/ Pankaj Roy
411	4th	Eng v WI	Edgbaston	1957	P.B.H. May/ M.C. Cowdrey
405	5th	Aus v Eng	Sydney	1946-47	S.G. Barnes/ D.G. Bradman
399	4th	WI v Eng	Bridgetown	1959-60	G.S. Sobers/ F.M.M. Worrell
397	3rd	Pak v SL	Faisalabad	1985-86	Qasim Omar/ Javed Miandad
388	4th	Aus v Eng	Headingley	1934	W.H. Ponsford/ D.G. Bradman
387	1st	NZ v WI	Georgetown	1971-72	G.M. Turner/ T.W. Jarvis
382	2nd	Eng v Aus	The Oval	1938	L. Hutton/ M. Leyland
382	1st	Aus v WI	Bridgetown	1964-65	W.M. Lawry/ R.B. Simpson
370	3rd	Eng v SA	Lord's	1947	W.J. Edrich/ D.C.S. Compton
369	2nd	Eng v NZ	Headingley	1965	J.H. Edrich/ K.F. Barrington
359	1st	Eng v SA	Johannesburg	1948-49	L. Hutton/ C. Washbrook
351	2nd	Eng v Aus	The Oval	1985	G.A. Gooch/ D.I. Gower
350	4th	Pak v NZ	Dunedin	1972-73	Mushtaq Mohammad/ Asif Iqbal
347	7th	WI v Aus	Bridgetown	1954-55	D.S. Atkinson/ C.C. Depeiza
346	6th	Aus v Eng	Melbourne	1936-37	J.H.W. Fingleton/ D.G. Bradman
344*	2nd	Ind v WI	Calcutta	1978-79	S.M. Gavaskar/ D.B. Vengsarkar
341	3rd	SA v Aus	Adelaide	1963-64	E.J. Barlow/ R.G Pollock

Runs	Wkt	Teams	Venue	Year	Batsmen
338	3rd	WI v Eng	Port of Spain	1953-54	E.D. Weekes/ F.M.M. Worrell
336	4th	Aus v WI	Sydney	1968-69	W.M. Lawry/ K.D. Walters
332*	5th	Aus v Eng	Headingley	1993	A.R. Border/ S.R. Waugh
331	2nd	Eng v Aus	Edgbaston	1985	R.T. Robinson/ D.I. Gower
329	1st	Aus v Eng	Trent Bridge	1989	G.R. Marsh/ M.A. Taylor
323	1st	Eng v Aus	Melbourne	1911-12	J.B. Hobbs/ W. Rhodes
322	4th	Pak v Eng	Edgbaston	1992	Javed Miandad/ Salim Malik
319	3rd	SA v Eng	Trent Bridge	1947	A. Melville/ A.D. Nourse
316[1]	3rd	Ind v Eng	Madras	1981-82	G.R. Viswanath/ Yashpal Sharma
308	7th	Pak v Ind	Lahore	1955-56	Waqar Hassan/ Imtiaz Ahmed
308	3rd	WI v Aus	St Johns	1983-84	R.B. Richardson/ I.V.A. Richards
308	3rd	Eng v Ind	Lord's	1990	G.A. Gooch/ A.J. Lamb
303	3rd	WI v Eng	Trent Bridge	1976	I.V.A. Richards/ A.I. Kallicharran
301	2nd	Aus v Eng	Headingley	1948	A.R. Morris/ D.G. Bradman

[1] D.B. Vengsarkar retired hurt and was succeeded by Yashpal Sharma when the score was 99. In all 415 runs were scored for the 3rd wicket.

LEADING TEST MATCH
WICKET TAKERS

Name	Team	Balls	Runs	Wkts	Avg	B/B	5WI	10WM	S/R
Kapil Dev	Ind	27590	12795	432	29.61	9-83	23	2	63.86
R.J. Hadlee	NZ	21918	9611	431	22.29	9-52	36	9	50.85
I.T. Botham	Eng	21815	10878	383	28.40	8-34	27	4	56.95
M.D. Marshall	WI	17585	7876	376	20.94	7-22	22	4	46.76
Imran Khan	Pak	19458	8258	362	22.81	8-58	23	6	53.75
D.K. Lillee	Aus	18467	8493	355	23.92	7-83	23	7	52.01
R.G.D. Willis	Eng	17357	8190	325	25.20	8-43	16	0	53.40
L.R. Gibbs	WI	27115	8989	309	29.09	8-38	18	2	87.75
F.S. Trueman	Eng	15178	6625	307	21.57	8-31	17	3	49.43
D.L. Underwood	Eng	21862	7674	297	25.83	8-51	17	6	73.60
B.S. Bedi	Ind	21367	7637	266	28.71	7-98	14	1	80.32
J. Garner	WI	13169	5433	259	20.97	6-56	7	0	50.84
J.B. Statham	Eng	16056	6261	252	24.84	7-39	9	1	63.71
M.A. Holding	WI	12680	5898	249	23.68	8-92	13	2	50.92
R. Benaud	Aus	19108	6704	248	27.03	7-72	16	1	77.04
G.D. McKenzie	Aus	17681	7328	246	29.78	8-71	16	3	71.87
B.S. Chandrasekhar	Ind	15963	7199	242	29.74	8-79	16	2	65.96
A.V. Bedser	Eng	15918	5876	236	24.89	7-44	15	5	67.44
Abdul Qadir	Pak	17126	7742	236	32.80	9-56	15	5	72.56
G.S. Sobers	WI	21599	7999	235	34.03	6-73	6	0	91.91
R.R. Lindwall	Aus	13650	5251	228	23.03	7-38	12	0	59.86
C. McDermott	Aus	12630	6324	224	28.23	8-97	9	2	56.38
Wasim Akram	Pak	12014	5203	222	23.43	7-119	15	3	54.11
C.V. Grimmett	Aus	14513	5231	216	24.21	7-40	21	7	67.18
M. Hughes	Aus	11865	5780	208	27.78	8-87	7	1	57.04
C.A. Walsh	WI	11826	5178	203	25.50	6-62	5	1	58.25
J.A. Snow	Eng	12021	5387	202	26.66	7-40	8	1	59.50
A.M.E. Roberts	WI	11135	5174	202	25.61	7-54	11	2	55.12
J.R. Thomson	Aus	10535	5601	200	28.00	6-46	8	0	52.67

BEST BOWLING IN A TEST MATCH INNINGS

10-53	J.C. Laker	England v Australia	Old Trafford	1956
9-28	G.A. Lohmann	England v S. Africa	Johannesburg	1895-96
9-37	J.C. Laker	England v Australia	Old Trafford	1956
9-52	R.J. Hadlee	N Zealand v Australia	Brisbane	1985-86
9-56	Abdul Qadir	Pakistan v England	Lahore	1987-88
9-69	J.M. Patel	India v Australia	Kanpur	1959-60
9-83	Kapil Dev	India v W. Indies	Ahmedabad	1983-84
9-86	Sarfraz Nawaz	Pakistan v Australia	Melbourne	1978-79
9-95	J.M. Noreiga	W. Indies v India	Port of Spain	1970-71
9-102	S.P. Gupte	India v W. Indies	Kanpur	1958-59
9-103	S.F. Barnes	England v S. Africa	Johannesburg	1913-14
9-113	H.J. Tayfield	S. Africa v England	Johannesburg	1956-57
9-121	A.A. Mailey	Australia v England	Melbourne	1920-21
8-7	G.A. Lohmann	England v S. Africa	Port Elizabeth	1895-96
8-11	J. Briggs	England v S. Africa	Cape Town	1888-89
8-29	S.F. Barnes	England v S. Africa	The Oval	1912
8-29	C.E.H. Croft	W. Indies v Pakistan	Port of Spain	1976-77
8-31	F. Laver	Australia v England	Old Trafford	1909
8-31	F.S. Trueman	England v India	Old Trafford	1952
8-34	I.T. Botham	England v Pakistan	Lord's	1978
8-35	G.A. Lohmann	England v Australia	Sydney	1886-87
8-38	L.R. Gibbs	W. Indies v India	Bridgetown	1961-62
8-43	A.E. Trott	Australia v England	Adelaide	1894-95
8-43	H. Verity	England v Australia	Lord's	1934
8-43	R.G.D. Willis	England v Australia	Headingley	1981
8-45	C.E.L. Ambrose	W. Indies v England	Bridgetown	1989-90

MOST DISMISSALS BY A WICKET-KEEPER IN TEST MATCHES

Player	Team	Tests	Cat	St	Total	DPM
R.W. Marsh	Aus	96	343	12	355	3.69
P.J.L. Dujon	WI	81	267	5	272[1]	3.35
A.P.E. Knott	Eng	95	250	19	269	2.83
Wasim Bari	Pak	81	201	27	228	2.81
T.G. Evans	Eng	91	173	46	219	2.40
I.A. Healy	Aus	59	186	14	200	3.38
S.M.H. Kirmani	Ind	88	160	38	198	2.25
D.L. Murray	WI	62	181	8	189	3.04
A.T.W. Grout	Aus	51	163	24	187	3.66
I.D.S. Smith	NZ	63	168	8	176	2.79
R.W. Taylor	Eng	57	167	7	174	3.05
J.H.B. Waite	SA	50	124	17	141	2.82
W.A.S. Oldfield	Aus	54	78	52	130	2.40
K.S. More	Ind	49	110	20	130	2.65
J.M. Parks	Eng	46	103	11	114[2]	2.47
Salim Yousuf	Pak	32	91	13	104	3.25

[1] Includes 2 catches in 2 Tests when not keeping wicket [2] Includes 2 catches in 3 Tests when not keeping wicket

MOST TEST MATCH CATCHES

Player	Team	Catches	Opposition								
			Aus	Eng	Ind	NZ	Pak	SA	SL	WI	Zim
A.R. Border	Aus	152	-	57	14	31	22	1	8	19	0
G.S. Chappell	Aus	122	-	61	5	18	22	0	0	16	0
I.V.A. Richards	WI	122	24	29	39	7	23	0	0	-	0
I.T. Botham	Eng	120	61	-	14	14	14	0	2	15	0
M.C. Cowdrey	Eng	120	40	-	11	15	11	22	0	21	0
R.B. Simpson	Aus	110	-	30	21	0	3	27	0	29	0
W.R. Hammond	Eng	110	43	-	6	9	4	30	0	22	0
G.S. Sobers	WI	109	27	40	27	11	19	0	0	-	0
S.M. Gavaskar	Ind	108	19	35	-	11	6	0	7	17	0
I.M. Chappell	Aus	105	-	31	17	16	6	11	0	24	0

CURRENT PLAYERS' CAPTAINCY RECORDS

Player	Team	Tests	Won	Drawn	Lost	Tied
M.A. Atherton	Eng	2	1	0	1	0
M. Azharuddin	Ind	27	9	11	7	0
A.R. Border	Aus	90	31	37	21	1
W.J. Cronje	SA	1	0	0	1	0
M.D. Crowe	NZ	16	2	7	7	0
P.A. De Silva	SL	4	0	2	2	0
A. Flower	Zim	3	0	1	2	0
G.A. Gooch	Eng	34	10	12	12	0
D.L. Haynes	WI	4	1	2	1	0
D.L. Houghton	Zim	4	0	2	2	0
Javed Miandad	Pak	34	14	14	6	0
A.H. Jones	NZ	1	0	0	1	0
Kapil Dev	Ind	34	4	22	7	1
A. Ranatunga	SL	22	2	12	8	0
R.B. Richardson	WI	10	5	4	1	0
K.R. Rutherford	NZ	2	0	0	2	0
Salim Malik	Pak	3	2	0	1	0
A.J. Stewart	Eng	2	0	0	2	0
Waqar Younis	Pak	1	1	0	0	0
Wasim Akram	Pak	5	1	2	2	0
K.C. Wessels	SA	10	3	6	1	0

COOPERS & LYBRAND WORLD RATINGS

First introduced in 1987, the Coopers & Lybrand ratings
are generally considered to be the most reliable assessment of a cricketer's current form. Whereas a player's
Test average provides a fixed record of every match
played over his entire Test career, the Coopers and
Lybrand ratings can indicate both when a player was at
his best and who is performing at the highest level at any
given time. The first figure featured in every players'
profile is their current position in the world ranking. The
second figure is their current points' total. For the more
established Test players the maximum number of
obtainable points is 1000. However if a player has not
played enough innings or taken enough wickets their
points' total is limited and they are given a provisional
figure only. Each player with a provisional figure is
indicated by an asterisk. The maximum points available to
each player are indicated below.

Batsmen

Test innings played	Maximum rating possible
1	430 points
10	700 points
20	1000 points

Bowlers

Test wickets taken	Maximum rating possible
10	400 points
30	800 points
50	1000 points

Any player that misses a Test match, for whatever reason,
automatically loses 1% of his ratings' total. Players absent
with a long term injury will therefore return with a lower
rating regardless of how well they performed before they
were injured.
All Coopers & Lybrand ratings are correct up to and
including the Third Test between India and Sri Lanka in
February 1994.

COOPERS & LYBRAND WORLD RATINGS - TEST BATSMEN

Rank	Player	Team	Rating
1	G.A. Gooch	England	819
2	D.L. Haynes	West Indies	818
3	R.B. Richardson	West Indies	785
4	S.R. Tendulkar	India	765
5	D.C. Boon	Australia	725
6	B.C. Lara	West Indies	696 *
7	Salim Malik	Pakistan	685
8	S.R. Waugh	Australia	676
9	V.G. Kambli	India	673 *
10	M. Azharuddin	India	658
11	N.S. Sidhu	India	657
12	M.A. Taylor	Australia	652
13	M.D. Crowe	New Zealand	651
14	Shoaib Mohammad	Pakistan	640
15	A.R. Border	Australia	625
16	R.A. Smith	England	611
17	A.C. Hudson	South Africa	604
18	W.J. Cronje	South Africa	602 *
19	Javed Miandad	Pakistan	599
20=	J.G. Wright	New Zealand	598
	M.J. Slater	Australia	598 *
22	K.C. Wessels	South Africa	595 *
23	R.S. Mahanama	Sri Lanka	589
24=	M.A. Atherton	England	583
	K.R. Rutherford	New Zealand	583
26	M.E. Waugh	Australia	568
27	A.J. Stewart	England	567
28	H.P. Tillekeratne	Sri Lanka	565
29	P.A. de Silva	Sri Lanka	564
30	C.L. Hooper	West Indies	557
31	G.A. Hick	England	554
32=	P.V. Simmons	West Indies	549
	A.H. Jones	New Zealand	549
34	J.N. Rhodes	South Africa	548 *
35	D.M. Jones	Australia	525
36	S.T. Jayasuriya	Sri Lanka	515
37	A.D.R. Campbell	Zimbabwe	513 *
38	A. Ranatunga	Sri Lanka	511
39	A. Flower	Zimbabwe	502 *
40=	Asif Mujtaba	Pakistan	486
	S.V. Manjrekar	India	486
42	K.L.T. Arthurton	West Indies	483
43	G. Kirsten	South Africa	479 *
44	A.P. Gurusinha	Sri Lanka	474
45	Inzamam-ul-Haq	Pakistan	472 *
46	Kapil Dev	India	468
47	R.J. Shastri	India	454
48	M.J. Greatbatch	New Zealand	442
49	I.A. Healy	Australia	437
50	Basit Ali	Pakistan	428 *

COOPERS & LYBRAND WORLD RATINGS - TEST BOWLERS

Rank	Player	Team	Rating
1	Waqar Younis	Pakistan	909
2	A.R. Kumble	India	890
3	C.E.L. Ambrose	West Indies	888
4	S.K. Warne	Australia	877
5	A.A. Donald	South Africa	817
6	I.R. Bishop	West Indies	802
7	C.J. McDermott	Australia	701
8	W.K.M. Benjamin	West Indies	697 *
9	M.G. Hughes	Australia	683
10=	A.R.C. Fraser	England	674
	Wasim Akram	Pakistan	674
12	M. Muralitharan	Sri Lanka	643
13	B.A. Reid	Australia	615
14	Kapil Dev	India	605
15	B.N. Schultz	South Africa	600 *
16	C.A. Walsh	West Indies	595
17	S.L.V. Raju	India	574
18	M. Prabhakar	India	559
19	T.B.A. May	Australia	548
20	P.A.J. DeFreitas	England	531
21	D.K. Morrison	New Zealand	493
22	P.R. Reiffel	Australia	468 *
23	P.C.R. Tufnel	England	449
24	K.P.J. Warnaweera	Sri Lanka	429 *
25	D.E. Malcolm	England	428
26	B.P. Patterson	West Indies	412
27	M.R. Whitney	Australia	399 *
28	C.P.H. Ramanayake	Sri Lanka	382 *
29	C.C. Lewis	England	381
30	D.H. Brain	Zimbabwe	375 *
31	Maninder Singh	India	362
32=	N.A. Foster	England	355
	Tausif Ahmed	Pakistan	355
	R.K. Chauhan	India	355 *
35	W. Watson	New Zealand	346 *
36	J. Srinath	India	339 *
37	S.D. Anurasiri	Sri Lanka	337 *
38	D.N. Patel	New Zealand	336 *
39	A.I.C. Dodemaide	Australia	330 *
40	R.J. Shastri	India	324
41	R.A. Harper	West Indies	317 *
42	M.L. Su'a	New Zealand	313 *
43	B.M. McMillan	South Africa	297 *
44	Mushtaq Ahmed	Pakistan	283 *
45	R.P. Snell	South Africa	278 *
46=	Aqib Javed	Pakistan	259 *
	P.M. Such	England	259 *
48	J.E. Emburey	England	252 *
49=	G.R.J. Matthews	Australia	249
	M.E. Waugh	Australia	249 *
	U.C. Hathurusinghe	Sri Lanka	249 *

AAMIR SOHAIL

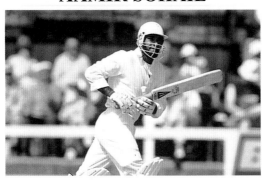

Full name: Aamir Sohail
Born: 14/09/66 Lahore, Pakistan
Country: Pakistan
Left-hand opening batsman - Left-arm slow bowler
Test debut: 04/06/92 v England - Edgbaston, Birmingham

Test Career Record: *Batting & Fielding*

MAT	Inns	N/O	Runs	H/S	Avg	100s	50s	Cat
14	26	1	799	205	31.96	1	5	10

Test Career Record: *Bowling*

Balls	Runs	Wkts	Avg	Best	5WI	10WM	BPW
168	101	2	50.50	1-14	0	0	84.00

Overseas tours: Aus 91/92, 92/93, Eng 92, NZ 92/93, 93/94, WI 92/93, SA 92/93, Zim 92/93, Sharjah 90/91, 91/92, 93/94, WC: Aus & NZ 91/92, Pak B: Zim 86/87, Pak A: SL 90/91

Test matches: Eng 92 (5), NZ 92/93 (1), WI 92/93 (2), Zim 93/94 (3), NZ 93/94 (3)

Highest score against each country:			100s	50s
England	205	Old Trafford 92	1	1
New Zealand	78	Auckland 93/94	0	2
West Indies	55	Port of Spain 92/93	0	1
Zimbabwe	63	Karachi 93/94	0	1

Coopers & Lybrand world rating (batting): 53 (414)

CURTLY AMBROSE

Full name: Curtly Elconn Lynwall Ambrose
Born: 21/09/63 Swetes Village, Antigua
Country: West Indies
Right-arm fast bowler - Left-hand lower order batsman
Test debut: 02/04/88 v Pakistan - Bourda, Georgetown

Test Career Record: *Batting & Fielding*								
MAT	Inns	N/O	Runs	H/S	Avg	100s	50s	Cat
43	64	13	589	53	11.54	0	1	9

Test Career Record: *Bowling*							
Balls	Runs	Wkts	Avg	Best	5WI	10WM	BPW
10462	4097	193	21.22	8-45	9	2	54.20

Overseas tours: Eng 88, 91, Aus 88/89, 91/92, 92/93, Ind 89/90, 93/94, Pak 90/91, 91/92, SA 92/93, S/L 93/94, Sharjah 88/89, 89/90, 91/92, 93/94, WC: Aus & NZ 91/92

Test matches: Pak 87/88 (3), Eng 88 (5), Aus 88/89 (5), Ind 88/89 (4), Eng 89/90 (3), Pak 90/91 (3), Aus 90/91 (5), Eng 91 (5), SA 91/92 (1), Aus 92/93 (5), Pak 92/93 (3), SL 93/94 (1)

Best bowling against each country:			5WI	10WM
Australia	7-25	Perth 92/93	4	1
England	8-45	Bridgetown 89/90	3	1
India	3-66	Bridgetown 88/89	0	0
Pakistan	5-35	Lahore 90/91	1	0
South Africa	6-34	Bridgetown 91/92	1	0
Sri Lanka	3-14	Moratuwa 93/94	0	0

Coopers & Lybrand world rating (bowling): 3 (888)

PRAVIN AMRE

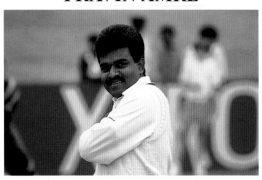

Full name: Pravin Kalyan Amre
Born: 14/08/68 Bombay, India
Country: India
Right-hand middle order batsman
Test debut: 13/11/92 v South Africa - Kingsmead, Durban

Test Career Record:	*Batting & Fielding*							
MAT	Inns	N/O	Runs	H/S	Avg	100s	50s	Cat
11	13	3	425	103	42.50	1	3	9

Overseas tours: Zim 92/93, SA 92/93, SL 93/94, WC: Aus & NZ 91/92

Test matches: SA 92/93 (4), Eng 92/93 (3), Zim 92/93 (1), SL 93/94 (3)

Highest score against each country:			100s	50s
England	78	Madras 92/93	0	2
South Africa	103	Durban 92/93	1	0
Sri Lanka	21	Colombo 93/94	0	0
	21	Colombo 93/94		
Zimbabwe	52*	Delhi 92/93	0	1

Coopers & Lybrand world rating (batting): 65= (343)*

KEVIN ARNOTT

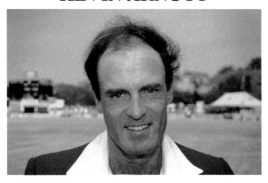

Full name: Kevin John Arnott
Born: 08/03/61 Salisbury (Harare), Zimbabwe
Country: Zimbabwe
Right-hand opening batsman
Test debut: 18/10/92 v India - Harare Sports Club

Test Career Record: *Batting & Fielding*

MAT	Inns	N/O	Runs	H/S	Avg	100s	50s	Cat
4	8	1	302	101*	43.14	1	1	4

Overseas tours: Eng 90, 93, Ind 92/93, Sharjah 92/93, WC: Ind 87/88, Aus & NZ: 91/92

Test matches: Ind 92/93 (1), NZ 92/93 (2), Ind 92/93 (1)

Highest score against each country:			100s	50s
India	40	Harare 92/93	0	0
New Zealand	101*	Bulawayo 92/93	1	1

Coopers & Lybrand world rating (batting): 77 (253)*

KEITH ARTHURTON

Full name: Keith Lloyd Thomas Arthurton
Born: 21/02/65 Charlestown, Nevis
Country: West Indies
Left-hand middle order batsman - Left-arm slow bowler
Test debut: 21/07/88 v England - Headingley, Leeds

Test Career Record: *Batting & Fielding*

MAT	Inns	N/O	Runs	H/S	Avg	100s	50s	Cat
15	24	3	641	157*	30.52	1	4	10

Test Career Record: *Bowling*

Balls	Runs	Wkts	Avg	Best	5WI	10WM	BPW
162	68	0	-	-	-	-	-

Overseas tours: Eng 88, Aus 88/89, 91/92, 92/93, Ind 89/90, 93/94, Pak 91/92, SL 93/94, Sharjah 88/89, 89/90, 91/92, 93/94, WC: Aus & NZ 91/92

Test matches: Eng 88 (1), Ind 88/89 (4), SA 91/92 (1), Aus 92/93 (5), Pak 92/93 (3), SL 93/94 (1)

Highest score against each country:			100s	50s
Australia	157*	Brisbane 92/93	1	2
England	27	Headingley 88	0	0
India	37	Port of Spain 88/89	0	0
Pakistan	56	Bridgetown 92/93	0	1
South Africa	59	Bridgetown 91/92	0	1
Sri Lanka	0	Moratuwa 92/93	0	0

Coopers & Lybrand world rating (batting): 42 (483)

ASIF MUJTABA

Full name: Asif Mujtaba
Born: 04/11/67 Karachi, Pakistan
Country: Pakistan
Left-hand middle order batsman - Left-arm slow bowler
Test debut: 07/11/86 v West Indies - Gaddafi Stadium,
Lahore

Test Career Record: Batting & Fielding								
MAT	Inns	N/O	Runs	H/S	Avg	100s	50s	Cat
17	28	3	638	65*	25.52	0	7	14

Test Career Record: Bowling							
Balls	Runs	Wkts	Avg	Best	5WI	10WM	BPW
222	122	2	61.00	1-0	0	0	111.00

Overseas tours: Ind 86/87, Aus 86/87, Eng 87, 92, WI
92/93, NZ 92/93, 93/94, SA 92/93, Zim 92/93, Sharjah
86/87, 92/93, 93/94, Pak B: Zim 86/87

Test matches: WI 86/87 (2), Eng 87/88 (1), Eng 92 (5),
NZ 92/93 (1), WI 92/93 (3), Zim 93/94 (3), NZ 93/94 (2)

Highest score against each country:			100s	50s
England	59	Lord's 92	0	3
New Zealand	11	Hamilton 92/93	0	0
West Indies	59	St John's 92/93	0	1
Zimbabwe	65*	Lahore 93/94	0	3

Coopers & Lybrand world rating (batting): 40= (486)

MICHAEL ATHERTON

Full name: Michael Andrew Atherton
Born: 23/03/68 Manchester, Lancashire, England
Country: England
Right-hand opening batsman - Leg break bowler
Test debut: 10/08/89 v Australia - Trent Bridge,
Nottingham

Test Career Record: *Batting & Fielding*

MAT	Inns	N/O	Runs	H/S	Avg	100s	50s	Cat
29	55	1	1927	151	35.68	3	15	24

Test Career Record: *Bowling*

Balls	Runs	Wkts	Avg	Best	5WI	10WM	BPW
366	282	1	282.00	1-60	0	0	366.00

Overseas tours: Aus 90/91, NZ 90/91, Ind 92/93,
SL 92/93, WI 93/94, Eng A: Zim 89/90

Test matches: Aus 89 (2), NZ 90 (3), Ind 90 (3),
Aus 90/91 (5), WI 91 (5), Pak 92 (3), Ind 92/93 (1),
SL 92/93 (1), Aus 93 (6)

Highest score against each country:			100s	50s
Australia	105	Sydney 90/91	1	7
India	131	Old Trafford 90	1	3
New Zealand	151	Trent Bridge 90	1	3
Pakistan	76	Headingley 92	0	2
Sri Lanka	13	Colombo 92/93	0	0
West Indies	32	Trent Bridge 91	0	0

Coopers & Lybrand world rating (batting): 24= (583)

MOHAMMAD AZHARUDDIN

Full name: Mohammad Azharuddin
Born: 08/02/63 Hyderabad, India
Country: India
Right-hand middle order batsman - Right-arm medium bowler
Test debut: 31/12/84 v England - Eden Gardens, Calcutta

Test Career Record: *Batting & Fielding*

MAT	Inns	N/O	Runs	H/S	Avg	100s	50s	Cat
61	87	3	3957	199	47.10	14	12	60

Test Career Record: *Bowling*

Balls	Runs	Wkts	Avg	Best	5WI	10WM	BPW
7	12	0	-	-	-	-	-

Overseas tours: Aus 84/85, 85/86, 91/92, SL 85/86, 93/94, Eng 86, 90, WI 89/90, NZ 89/90, Pak 89/90, Zim 92/93, SA 92/93, Ban 88/89, Sharjah 84/85, 85/86, 86/87, 87/88, 88/89, 89/90, 91/92, WC: Aus & NZ 91/92, Young Ind: Zim 83/84

Test matches: Eng 84/85 (3), SL 85/86 (3), Aus 85/86 (3), Eng 86 (3), Aus 86/87 (3), SL 86/87 (1), Pak 86/87 (5), WI 87/88 (3), NZ 88/89 (3), WI 88/89 (3), Pak 89/90 (4), NZ 89/90 (3), Eng 90 (3), SL 90/91 (1), Aus 91/92 (5), Zim 92/93 (1), SA 92/93 (4), Eng 92/93 (3), Zim 92/93 (1), SL 93/94 (3), SL 93/94 (3)

Highest score against each country:			100s	50s
Australia	106	Adelaide 91/92	1	2
England	182	Calcutta 92/93	6	3
New Zealand	192	Auckland 89/90	1	1
Pakistan	141	Calcutta 86/87	3	2
South Africa	60	Port Elizabeth 92/93	0	1
Sri Lanka	199	Kanpur 86/87	3	1
West Indies	61	Bridgetown 88/89	0	2
Zimbabwe	42	Delhi 92/93	0	0

Coopers & Lybrand world rating (batting): 10 (658)

BASIT ALI

Full name: Basit Ali
Born: 13/12/70 Karachi, Pakistan
Country: Pakistan
Right-hand middle order batsman - Off break bowler
Test debut: 16/04/93 v West Indies - Queens Park Oval,
Port of Spain

Test Career Record: *Batting & Fielding*

MAT	Inns	N/O	Runs	H/S	Avg	100s	50s	Cat
9	15	1	652	103	46.57	1	4	4

Test Career Record: *Bowling*

Balls	Runs	Wkts	Avg	Best	5WI	10WM	BPW
6	6	0	-	-	-	-	-

Overseas tours: WI 92/93, Sharjah 93/94, NZ 93/94

Test matches: WI 92/93 (3), Zim 93/94 (3), NZ 93/94 (3)

Highest score against each country:			100s	50s
West Indies	92*	Bridgetown 92/93	0	2
New Zealand	103	Christchurch 93/94	1	2
Zimbabwe	40	Rawalpindi 93/94	0	0

Coopers & Lybrand world rating (batting): 50 (428)*

WINSTON BENJAMIN

Full name: Winston Keithroy Matthew Benjamin
Born: 31/12/64 All Saints, Antigua
Country: West Indies
Right-arm fast bowler - Right-hand lower order batsman
Test debut: 25/11/87 v India - Feroz Shah Kotla, Delhi

Test Career Record: *Batting & Fielding*

MAT	Inns	N/O	Runs	H/S	Avg	100s	50s	Cat
11	13	1	138	40*	11.50	0	0	5

Test Career Record: *Bowling*

Balls	Runs	Wkts	Avg	Best	5WI	10WM	BPW
1740	753	39	19.30	4-46	0	0	44.61

Overseas tours: Aus 86/87, 88/89, Pak 86/87, Ind 87/88, 89/90, 93/94, Eng 88, SL 93/94, Sharjah 86/87, 88/89, 89/90, 91/92, 93/94, WC: Ind & Pak 87/88, Aus & NZ 91/92, RW: Eng 85

Test matches: Ind 87/88 (1), Pak 87/88 (3), Eng 88 (3), Ind 88/89 (1), Pak 92/93 (2), SL 93/94 (1)

Best bowling against each country:			5WI	10WM
England	4-52	The Oval 88	0	0
India	1-17	Delhi 87/88	0	0
Pakistan	3-30	Bridgetown 92/93	0	0
Sri Lanka	4-46	Moratuwa 93/94	0	0

Coopers & Lybrand world rating (bowling): 8 (697)*

IAN BISHOP

Full name: Ian Raphael Bishop
Born: 24/10/67 Port of Spain, Trinidad
Country: West Indies
Right-arm fast bowler - Right-hand lower order batsman
Test debut: 25/03/89 v India - Bourda, Georgetown,
Guyana

Test Career Record: *Batting & Fielding*

MAT	Inns	N/O	Runs	H/S	Avg	100s	50s	Cat
18	28	8	231	30*	11.55	0	0	3

Test Career Record: *Bowling*

Balls	Runs	Wkts	Avg	Best	5WI	10WM	BPW
3912	1698	83	20.45	6-40	5	0	47.13

Overseas tours: Eng 88, 91, Aus 88/89, Aus 92/93,
Ind 89/90, Pak 90/91, 91/92, SA 92/93, Sharjah 88/89,
89/90, 91/92

Test matches: Ind 88/89 (3), Eng 89/90 (4), Pak 90/91
(3), Aus 92/93 (5), Pak 92/93 (3)

Best bowling against each country:			5WI	10WM
Australia	6-40	Perth 92/93	1	0
England	5-84	St John's 89/90	1	0
India	6-87	Bridgetown 88/89	1	0
Pakistan	5-41	Lahore 90/91	2	0

Coopers & Lybrand world rating (bowling): 6 (802)

TONY BLAIN

Full name: Tony Elston Blain
Born: 17/02/62 Nelson, New Zealand
Country: New Zealand
Right-hand middle order batsman - Wicket-Keeper
Test debut: 21/08/86 v England - The Oval, London

Test Career Record: *Batting & Fielding*									
MAT	*Inns*	*N/O*	*Runs*	*H/S*	*Avg*	*100s*	*50s*	*Cat*	*St*
11	20	3	456	78	26.82	0	2	18	2

Overseas tours: SL 85/86, Eng 86, Aus 87/88, 93/94, Ind 88/89, Sharjah 85/86, 87/88, Young NZ: Zim 88/89

Test matches: Eng 86 (1), Ind 88/89 (2), Aus 92/93 (2), Aus 93/94 (3), Pak 93/94 (3)

Highest score against each country:			100s	50s
Australia	51	Wellington 92/93	0	1
England	37	The Oval 86	0	0
India	16	Bombay 88/89	0	0
Pakistan	78	Wellington 93/94	0	1

Coopers & Lybrand world rating (batting): 63 (350)*

DAVID BOON

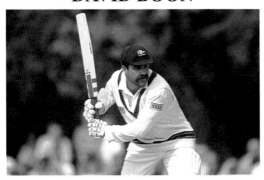

Full name: David Clarence Boon MBE
Born: 29/12/60 Launceston, Tasmania, Australia
Country: Australia
Right-hand opening/middle order batsman - Right-arm medium bowler
Test debut: 23/11/84 v West Indies - Wooloongabba, Brisbane

Test Career Record: *Batting & Fielding*

MAT	Inns	N/O	Runs	H/S	Avg	100s	50s	Cat
86	154	17	6287	200	45.89	18	28	82

Test Career Record: *Bowling*

Balls	Runs	Wkts	Avg	Best	5WI	10WM	BPW
18	5	0	-	-	-	-	-

Overseas tours: Eng 85, 89, 93, NZ 85/86, 89/90, Ind 86/87, 89/90, Pak 88/89, WI 90/91, Sharjah 85/86, 86/87, 89/90, WC: Ind & Pak 87/88, NZ 91/92

Test matches: WI 84/85 (3), Eng 85 (4), NZ 85/86 (3), Ind 85/86 (3), NZ 85/86 (3), Ind 86/87 (3), Eng 86/87 (4), NZ 87/88 (3), Eng 87/88 (1), SL 87/88 (1), Pak 88/89 (3), WI 88/89 (5), Eng 89 (6), NZ 89/90 (1), SL 89/90 (2), Pak 89/90 (2), NZ 89/90 (1), Eng 90/91 (5), WI 90/91 (5), Ind 91/92 (5), SL 92/93 (3), WI 92/93 (5), NZ 92/93 (3), Eng 93 (6), NZ 93/94 (3), SA 93/94 (3)

Highest score against each country:			100s	50s
England	184*	Sydney 87/88	6	8
India	135	Adelaide 91/92	6	2
New Zealand	200	Perth 89/90	3	8
Pakistan	43	Lahore 88/89	0	0
South Africa	50	Adelaide 93/94	0	1
Sri Lanka	68	Colombo 92/93	0	2
West Indies	149	Sydney 88/89	3	7

Coopers & Lybrand world rating (batting): 5 (725)

ALLAN BORDER

Full name: Allan Robert Border
Born: 27/07/55 Cremorne, Sydney, New South Wales, Australia
Country: Australia
Left-hand middle order batsman - Slow left-arm bowler
Test debut: 29/12/78 v England - Melbourne Cricket Ground

Test Career Record: *Batting & Fielding*							
MAT	Inns	N/O	Runs	H/S	Avg	100s	50s	Cat
153	260	43	11022	205	50.79	27	63	152

Test Career Record: *Bowling*						
Balls	Runs	Wkts	Avg	Best	5WI	10WM	BPW
3955	1508	39	38.66	7-46	2	1	101.41

Overseas tours: Ind 79/80, 84/85, 86/87, 89/90, Pak 79/80, 82/83, 88/89, Eng 80, 81, 85, 89, 93, SL 80/81, 82/83, 92/93, NZ 81/82, 85/86, 89/90, WI 83/84, 90/91, 92/93, Sharjah 84/85, 86/87, 89/90, WC: Eng 79, 83, Ind & Pak 87/88, NZ 91/92, RW: Eng 87

Test matches: Eng 78/79 (3), Pak 78/79 (2), Ind 79/80 (6), WI 79/80 (3), Eng 79/80 (3), Pak 79/80 (3), Eng 80 (1), NZ 80/81 (3), Ind 80/81 (3), Eng 81 (6), Pak 81/82 (3), WI 81/82 (3), NZ 81/82 (3), Pak 82/83 (3), Eng 82/83 (5), SL 82/83 (1), Pak 83/84 (5), WI 83/84 (5), WI 84/85 (5), Eng 85 (6), NZ 85/86 (3), Ind 85/86 (3), NZ 85/86 (3), Ind 86/87 (3), Eng 86/87 (5), NZ 87/88 (3), Eng 87/88 (1), SL 87/88 (1), Pak 88/89 (3), WI 88/89 (5), Eng 89 (6), NZ 89/90 (1), SL 89/90 (2), Pak 89/90 (3), NZ 89/90 (1), Eng 90/91 (5), WI 90/91 (5), Ind 91/92 (5), SL 92/93

(3), WI 92/93 (5), NZ 92/93 (3), Eng 93 (6), NZ 93/94
(3), SA 93/94 (3)

Highest score against each country:			100s	50s
England	200*	Headingley 93	8	21
India	163	Melbourne 85/86	4	9
New Zealand	205	Adelaide 87/88	5	6
Pakistan	153	Lahore 79/80	6	8
South Africa	84	Adelaide 93/94	0	1
Sri Lanka	106	Moratuwa 92/93	1	4
West Indies	126	Adelaide 81/82	3	14

Coopers & Lybrand world rating (batting): 15 (625)

DAVID BRAIN

Full name: David H Brain
Born: 04/10/64
Country: Zimbabwe
Left-arm medium bowler - Left-hand lower order batsman
Test debut: 07/11/92 v New Zealand - Harare Sports Club

Test Career Record: *Batting & Fielding*								
MAT	Inns	N/O	Runs	H/S	Avg	100s	50s	Cat
4	7	0	74	28	10.57	0	0	0
Test Career Record: *Bowling*								
Balls	Runs	Wkts	Avg		Best	5WI	10WM	BPW
978	431	18	23.94		5-42	1	0	54.33

Overseas tours: Ind 92/93, 93/94, Eng 93, Pak 93/94, Sharjah 92/93

Test matches: NZ 92/93 (1), Ind 92/93 (1), Pak 93/94 (2)

Best bowling against each country:			5WI	10WM
India	2-146	Delhi 92/93	0	0
New Zealand	3-49	Harare 92/93	0	0
Pakistan	5-42	Lahore 93/94	1	0

Coopers & Lybrand world rating (bowling): 30 (375)*

EDDO ANDRE BRANDES

Full name: Eddo André Brandes
Born: 05/03/63 Port Shepstone, Natal, South Africa
Country: Zimbabwe
Right-arm fast medium bowler - Right-hand lower order batsman
Test debut: 18/10/92 v India - Harare Sports Club

Test Career Record: *Batting & Fielding*

MAT	Inns	N/O	Runs	H/S	Avg	100s	50s	Cat
6	10	1	60	18	6.66	0	0	3

Test Career Record: *Bowling*

Balls	Runs	Wkts	Avg	Best	5WI	10WM	BPW
1264	598	17	35.17	3-45	0	0	74.35

Overseas tours: Eng 85, 90, 93, Ind 92/93, Pak 93/94, Sharjah 92/93, WC: Ind 87/88, Aus & NZ 91/92

Test matches: Ind 92/93 (1), NZ 92/93 (1), Ind 92/93 (1), Pak 93/94 (3)

Best bowling against each country:			5WI	10WM
India	0-3	Harare 92/93	0	0
New Zealand	2-49	Harare 92/93	0	0
Pakistan	3-45	Lahore 93/94	0	0

Coopers & Lybrand world rating (bowling): 59 (207)*

CHRIS CAIRNS

Full name: Christopher Lance Cairns
Born: 13/06/70 Picton, Marlborough, New Zealand
Country: New Zealand
Right-arm fast medium bowler - Right-hand middle order batsman
Test debut: 24/11/89 v Australia - W.A.C.A. Ground, Perth

Test Career Record: *Batting & Fielding*							
MAT	Inns	N/O	Runs	H/S	Avg	100s	50s	Cat
10	17	0	349	78	20.52	0	2	6

Test Career Record: *Bowling*						
Balls	Runs	Wkts	Avg	Best	5WI	10WM	BPW
1995	1207	28	43.10	6-52	2	0	71.25

Overseas tours: Aus 89/90, 93/94

Test matches: Aus 89/90 (1), SL 90/91 (1), Eng 91/92 (3), Aus 92/93 (2), Aus 93/94 (2), Pak 93/94 (1)

Best bowling against each country:			5WI	10WM
Australia	4-113	Perth 93/94	0	0
England	6-52	Auckland 91/92	1	0
Pakistan	2-75	Auckland 93/94	0	0
Sri Lanka	5-75	Auckland 90/91	1	0

Coopers & Lybrand world rating (bowling): 53= (244)*

ALISTAIR CAMPBELL

Full name: Alistair Douglas Ross Campbell
Born: 23/09/72 Salisbury (Harare), Zimbabwe
Country: Zimbabwe
Left-hand middle order batsman - Off break bowler
Test debut: 18/10/92 v India - Harare Sports Club

Test Career Record: *Batting & Fielding*								
MAT	Inns	N/O	Runs	H/S	Avg	100s	50s	Cat
7	13	1	478	75	39.83	0	5	5

Test Career Record: *Bowling*							
Balls	Runs	Wkts	Avg	Best	5WI	10WM	BPW
6	3	0	-	-	-	-	-

Overseas tours: Ind 92/93, 93/94, Eng 93, Pak 93/94, Sharjah 92/93, WC. Aus & NZ 91/92

Test matches: Ind 92/93 (1), NZ 92/93 (2), Ind 92/93 (1), Pak 93/94 (3)

Highest score against each country:			100s	50s
India	61	Delhi 92/93	0	1
New Zealand	52	Harare 92/93	0	1
Pakistan	75	Rawalpindi 93/94	0	3

Coopers & Lybrand world rating (batting): 37 (513)*

WESSEL CRONJE

Full name: Wessel Johannes Cronje
Born: 25/09/69 Bloemfontein, South Africa
Country: South Africa
Right-hand middle order batsman - Right-arm medium bowler
Test debut: 18/04/92 v West Indies - Kensington Oval, Bridgetown

Test Career Record: *Batting & Fielding*

MAT	Inns	N/O	Runs	H/S	Avg	100s	50s	Cat
10	18	2	614	135	38.37	2	2	4

Test Career Record: *Bowling*

Balls	Runs	Wkts	Avg	Best	5WI	10WM	BPW
712	196	4	49.00	2-17	0	0	178.00

Overseas tours: WI 91/92, SL 93/94, Ind 93/94, Aus 93/94, WC: Aus & NZ 91/92

Test matches: WI 91/92 (1), Ind 92/93 (3), SL 93/94 (3), Aus 93/94 (3)

Highest score against each country:			100s	50s
Australia	71	Melbourne 93/94	0	1
India	135	Port Elizabeth 92/93	1	0
Sri Lanka	122	Colombo 93/94	1	1
West Indies	5	Bridgetown 91/92	0	0

Coopers & Lybrand world rating (batting): 18 (602)*

MARTIN CROWE

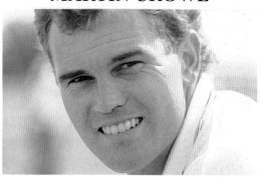

Full name: Martin David Crowe MBE
Born: 22/09/62 Henderson, Auckland, New Zealand
Country: New Zealand
Right-hand middle order batsman - Right-arm medium
bowler
Test debut: 26/02/81 v Australia - Basin Reserve,
Wellington

Test Career Record: *Batting & Fielding*

MAT	Inns	N/O	Runs	H/S	Avg	100s	50s	Cat
67	114	11	4850	299	47.08	15	16	61

Test Career Record: *Bowling*

Balls	Runs	Wkts	Avg	Best	5WI	10WM	BPW
1383	678	14	48.42	2-25	0	0	98.78

Overseas tours: Aus 82/83, 84/85, 85/86, 87/88, 89/90,
90/91, 93/94, Eng 83, 86, 90, SL 83/84, 84/85, 85/86, 86/
87, 92/93, Pak 84/85, 90/91, WI 84/85, Zim 92/93,
Sharjah 85/86, 89/90, WC: Ind 87/88, RW: Eng 85, 89

Test matches: Aus 81/82 (3), Eng 83 (4), Eng 83/84 (3),
SL 83/84 (3), Pak 84/85 (3), Pak 84/85 (3), WI 84/85 (4),
Aus 85/86 (3), Aus 85/86 (3), Eng 86 (3), WI 86/87 (3),
SL 86/87 (1), Aus 87/88 (3), Eng 87/88 (3), Pak 88/89 (2),
Aus 89/90 (1), Ind 89/90 (3), Eng 90 (3), Pak 90/91 (3),
SL 90/91 (2), Eng 91/92 (3), Zim 92/93 (2), SL 92/93 (2),
Aus 92/93 (3), Aus 93/94 (1)

Highest score against each country:			100s	50s
Australia	188	Brisbane 85/86	3	6
England	143	Wellington 87/88	3	2
India	113	Auckland 89/90	1	0
Pakistan	174	Wellington 88/89	2	6
Sri Lanka	299	Wellington 90/91	2	0
West Indies	188	Georgetown 84/85	3	1
Zimbabwe	140	Harare 92/93	1	1

Coopers & Lybrand world rating (batting): 13 (651)

DARYLL CULLINAN

Full name: Daryll John Cullinan
Born: 04/03/67 Kimberley, South Africa
Country: South Africa
Right-hand middle order batsman - Off break bowler
Test debut: 02/01/93 v India - Newlands, Cape Town

Test Career Record: *Batting & Fielding*								
MAT	Inns	N/O	Runs	H/S	Avg	100s	50s	Cat
7	12	0	337	102	28.08	1	1	2

Overseas tours: SL 93/94, Ind 93/94, Aus 93/94

Test matches: Ind 92/93 (1), SL 93/94 (3), Aus 93/94 (3)

Highest score against each country:			100s	50s
Australia	10	Adelaide 93/94	0	0
India	46	Cape Town 92/93	0	0
Sri Lanka	102	Colombo 93/94	1	1

Coopers & Lybrand world rating (batting): 74 (280)*

ARAVINDA DE SILVA

Full name: Pinnaduwage Aravinda De Silva
Born: 17/10/65 Colombo, Sri Lanka
Country: Sri Lanka
Right-hand middle order batsman - Off break bowler
Test debut: 23/08/84 v England - Lord's, London

Test Career Record: *Batting & Fielding*

MAT	Inns	N/O	Runs	H/S	Avg	100s	50s	Cat
41	70	3	2616	267	39.04	6	12	20

Test Career Record: *Bowling*

Balls	Runs	Wkts	Avg	Best	5WI	10WM	BPW
732	384	11	34.90	3-39	0	0	66.54

Overseas tours: Eng 84, 88, 90, 91, Aus 84/85, 87/88, 89/90, Pak 85/86, 91/92, Ind 86/87, 89/90, 90/91, 93/94, NZ 90/91, Ban 88/89, Sharjah 83/84, 85/86, 86/87, 87/88, 88/89, 89/90, 90/91, 92/93, 93/94, WC: Ind & Pak 87/88, Aus & NZ 91/92

Test matches: Eng 84 (1), Ind 85/86 (3), Pak 85/86 (3), Pak 85/86 (3), Ind 86/87 (3), Aus 87/88 (1), Eng 88 (1), Aus 89/90 (2), Ind 90/91 (1), NZ 90/91 (3), Eng 91 (1), Pak 91/92 (3), Aus 92/93 (3), NZ 92/93 (2), Eng 92/93(1), Ind 93/94 (3), SA 93/94 (3), WI 93/94 (1), Ind 93/94 (3)

Highest score against each country:			100s	50s
Australia	167	Brisbane 89/90	1	4
England	80	Colombo 92/93	0	1
India	148	Colombo 93/94	1	2
New Zealand	267	Wellington 90/91	2	2
Pakistan	122	Faisalabad 85/86	2	0
South Africa	82	Colombo 93/94	0	2
West Indies	53	Moratuwa 93/94	0	1

Coopers & Lybrand world rating (batting): 29 (564)

PHILLIP DEFREITAS

Full name: Phillip Anthony Jason DeFreitas
Born: 18/02/66 Scotts Head, Dominica
Country: England
Right-arm fast medium bowler - Right-hand middle order batsman
Test debut: 14/11/86 v Australia - Woolloongabba, Brisbane

Test Career Record: *Batting & Fielding*

MAT	Inns	N/O	Runs	H/S	Avg	100s	50s	Cat
33	50	4	562	55*	12.21	0	1	9

Test Career Record: *Bowling*

Balls	Runs	Wkts	Avg	Best	5WI	10WM	BPW
7030	3218	95	33.87	7-70	3	0	74.00

Overseas tours: Aus 86/87, 87/88, 90/91, NZ 87/88, 90/91, 91/92, Pak 87/88, Ind 89/90, 92/93, WI 89/90, SL 92/93, Sharjah 86/87, WC: Ind & Pak 87/88, Aus & NZ 91/92

Test matches: Aus 86/87 (4), Pak 87 (1), Pak 87/88 (2), NZ 87/88 (2), WI 88 (3), Aus 89 (1), WI 89/90 (2), NZ 90 (2), Aus 90/91 (3), WI 91 (5), SL 91 (1), NZ 91/92 (3), Pak 92 (2), Ind 92/93 (1), Aus 93 (1)

Best bowling against each country:			5WI	10WM
Australia	4-56	Adelaide 90/91	0	0
India	0-75	Bombay 92/93	0	0
New Zealand	5-53	Trent Bridge 90	1	0
Pakistan	5-86	Karachi 87/88	1	0
Sri Lanka	7-70	Lord's 91	1	0
West Indies	4-34	Headingley 91	0	0

Coopers & Lybrand world rating (bowling): 20 (531)

ALLAN DONALD

Full name: Allan Anthony Donald
Born: 20/10/66 Bloemfontein, South Africa
Country: South Africa
Right-arm fast bowler - Right-hand lower order batsman
Test debut: 18/04/92 v West Indies - Kensington Oval, Bridgetown

Test Career Record: *Batting & Fielding*

MAT	Inns	N/O	Runs	H/S	Avg	100s	50s	Cat
11	14	8	45	14*	7.50	0	0	2

Test Career Record: *Bowling*

Balls	Runs	Wkts	Avg	Best	5WI	10WM	BPW
2696	1143	51	22.41	7-84	3	1	52.86

Overseas tours: Ind 91/92, 93/94, WI 91/92, SL 93/94, Aus 93/94, WC: Aus & NZ 91/92

Test matches: WI 91/92 (1), Ind 92/93 (4), SL 93/94 (3), Aus 93/94 (3)

Best bowling against each country:			5WI	10WM
Australia	4-83	Sydney 93/94	0	0
India	7-84	Port Elizabeth 92/93	2	1
Sri Lanka	5-69	Moratuwa 93/94	1	0
West Indies	4-77	Bridgetown 91/92	0	0

Coopers & Lybrand world rating (bowling): 5 (817)

ANDREW FLOWER

Full name: Andrew Flower
Born: 20/04/68 Cape Town, South Africa
Country: Zimbabwe
Left-hand middle order batsman - Wicket-Keeper
Test debut: 18/10/92 v India - Harare Sports Club

Test Career Record: *Batting & Fielding*

MAT	Inns	N/O	Runs	H/S	Avg	100s	50s	Cat	St
7	12	3	499	115	55.44	1	5	14	2

Test Career Record: *Bowling*

Balls	Runs	Wkts	Avg	Best	5WI	10WM	BPW
1	0	0	-	-	-	-	-

Overseas tours: Ind 92/93, 93/94, Eng 93, Pak 93/94, Sharjah 92/93, WC: Aus & NZ 91/92

Test matches: Ind 92/93 (1), NZ 92/93 (2), Ind 92/93 (1), Pak 93/94 (3)

Highest score against each country:			100s	50s
India	115	Delhi 92/93	1	2
New Zealand	81	Bulawayo 92/93	0	1
Pakistan	63	Karachi 93/94	0	2

Coopers & Lybrand world rating (batting): 39 (502)*

GRANT FLOWER

Full name: Grant William Flower
Born: 20/12/70 Salisbury (Harare), Zimbabwe
Country: Zimbabwe
Right-hand middle order batsman - Left-arm slow bowler
Test debut: 18/10/92 v India - Harare Sports Club

Test Career Record: *Batting & Fielding*								
MAT	Inns	N/O	Runs	H/S	Avg	100s	50s	Cat
7	13	0	343	96	26.38	0	2	1
Test Career Record: *Bowling*								
Balls	Runs	Wkts	Avg		Best	5WI	10WM	BPW
282	144	2	72.00		1-8	0	0	141.00

Overseas tours: Eng 90, 93, Ind 92/93, 93/94, Pak 93/94, Sharjah 92/93

Test matches: Ind 92/93 (1), NZ 92/93 (2), Ind 92/93 (1), Pak 93/94 (3)

Highest score against each country:			100s	50s
India	96	Delhi 92/93	0	2
New Zealand	45	Bulawayo 92/93	0	0
Pakistan	30	Lahore 93/94	0	0

Coopers & Lybrand world rating (batting): 73 (289)*

ANGUS FRASER

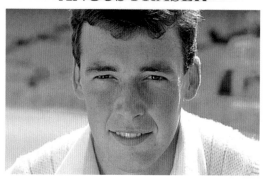

Full name: Angus Robert Charles Fraser
Born: 08/08/65 Billinge, Lancashire, England
Country: England
Right-arm fast medium bowler - Right-hand lower order batsman
Test debut: 06/07/89 v Australia - Edgbaston, Birmingham

Test Career Record: *Batting & Fielding*

MAT	Inns	N/O	Runs	H/S	Avg	100s	50s	Cat
12	16	1	129	29	8.60	0	0	2

Test Career Record: *Bowling*

Balls	Runs	Wkts	Avg	Best	5WI	10WM	BPW
3381	1386	55	25.20	6-82	5	0	61.47

Overseas tours: Ind 89/90, WI 89/90, 93/94, Aus 90/91, NZ 90/91

Test matches: Aus 89 (3), WI 89/90 (2), Ind 90 (3), Aus 90/91 (3), Aus 93 (1)

Best bowling against each country:			5WI	10WM
Australia	6-82	Melbourne 90/91	2	0
India	5-104	Lord's 90	2	0
West Indies	5-28	Kingston 89/90	1	0

Coopers & Lybrand world rating (bowling): 10 (674)

GRAHAM GOOCH

Full name: Graham Alan Gooch OBE
Born: 23/07/53 Whipps Cross, Leytonstone, Essex
Country: England
Right-hand opening batsman - Right-arm medium bowler
Test debut: 10/07/75 v Australia - Edgbaston

Test Career Record: *Batting & Fielding*

MAT	Inns	N/O	Runs	H/S	Avg	100s	50s	Cat
107	195	6	8293	333	43.87	19	45	99

Test Career Record: *Bowling*

Balls	Runs	Wkts	Avg	Best	5WI	10WM	BPW
2445	960	22	43.63	3-39	0	0	111.13

Overseas tours: Aus 78/79, 79/80, 90/91, Ind 79/80, 81/82, 89/90, 92/93, WI 80/81, 85/86, 89/90, SL 81/82, Pak 87/88, NZ 90/91, 91/92, WC: Ind & Pak 87/88, Aus & NZ 91/92

Test matches: Aus 75 (2), Pak 78 (2), NZ 78 (3), Aus 78/79 (6), Ind 79 (4), Aus 79/80 (2), Ind 79/80 (1), WI 80 (5), Aus 80 (1), WI 80/81 (4), Aus 81 (5), Ind 81/82 (6), SL 81/82 (1), Aus 85 (6), WI 85/86 (5), Ind 86 (3), NZ 86 (3), Pak 87/88 (3), WI 88 (5), SL 88 (1), Aus 89 (5), WI 89/90 (2), NZ 90 (3), Ind 90 (3), Aus 90/91 (4), WI 91 (5), SL 91 (1), NZ 91/92 (3), Pak 92 (5), Ind 92/93 (2), Aus 93 (6)

Highest score against each country:			100s	50s
Australia	196	The Oval 85	4	15
India	333	Lord's 90	5	8
New Zealand	183	Lord's 86	3	3
Pakistan	135	Headingley 92	1	5
Sri Lanka	174	Lord's 91	1	1
West Indies	154*	Headingley 91	5	13

Coopers & Lybrand world rating (batting): 1 (819)

MARK GREATBATCH

Full name: Mark John Greatbatch
Born: 11/12/63 Auckland, New Zealand
Country: New Zealand
Left-hand opening/middle order batsman - Wicket-Keeper
Test debut: 25/02/88 v England - Eden Park, Auckland

Test Career Record: *Batting & Fielding*								
MAT	Inns	N/O	Runs	H/S	Avg	100s	50s	Cat
32	57	5	1798	146*	34.57	3	9	25

Test Career Record: *Bowling*							
Balls	Runs	Wkts	Avg	Best	5WI	10WM	BPW
6	0	0	-	-	-	-	-

Overseas tours: Ind 88/89, Aus 89/90, 90/91, 93/94, Eng 90, Pak 90/91, Zim 92/93, Sharjah 87/88, 89/90, RW: Eng 88, 90, 92, Young NZ: Zim 88/89

Test matches: Eng 87/88 (2), Ind 88/89 (3), Pak 88/89 (1), Aus 89/90 (1), Ind 89/90 (3), Aus 89/90 (1), Eng 90 (3), Pak 90/91 (3), SL 90/91 (2), Eng 91/92 (1), Zim 92/93 (2), Pak 92/93 (1), Aus 92/93 (3), Aus 93/94 (3), Pak 93/94 (3)

Highest score against each country:			100s	50s
Australia	146*	Perth 89/90	1	2
England	107*	Auckland 87/88	1	1
India	90	Hyderabad 88/89	0	1
Pakistan	133	Hamilton 92/93	1	1
Sri Lanka	65	Auckland 90/91	0	1
Zimbabwe	88	Bulawayo 92/93	0	3

Coopers & Lybrand world rating (batting): 48 (442)

ASANKA GURUSINHA

Full name: Asanka Pradeep Gurusinha
Born: 16/09/66 Colombo, Sri Lanka
Country: Sri Lanka
Left-hand middle order batsman - Right-arm medium
bowler -Wicket-Keeper
Test debut: 07/11/85 v Pakistan - National Stadium,
Karachi

Test Career Record: *Batting & Fielding*

MAT	Inns	N/O	Runs	H/S	Avg	100s	50s	Cat
27	45	7	1500	137	39.47	4	4	20

Test Career Record: *Bowling*

Balls	Runs	Wkts	Avg	Best	5WI	10WM	BPW
1084	515	18	28.61	2-7	0	0	60.22

Overseas tours: Pak 85/86, 91/92, Ind 86/87, 89/90, 90/
91, Aus 87/88, 89/90, Eng 90, 91, NZ 90/91, Sharjah 85/
86, 86/87, 87/88, 89/90, 90/91, 92/93, 93/94, WC: Ind &
Pak 87/88, Aus & NZ 91/92
Test matches: Pak 85/86 (1), Pak 85/86 (2), Ind 86/87
(3), NZ 86/87 (1), Aus 89/90 (2), Ind 90/91 (1), NZ 90/91
(3), Eng 91 (1), Pak 91/92 (3), Aus 92/93 (3), NZ 92/93
(2), Eng 92/93 (1), Ind 93/94 (3), SA 93/94 (1)

Highest score against each country:			100s	50s
Australia	137	Colombo 92/93	1	0
England	43	Colombo 92/93	0	0
India	56	Colombo 93/94	0	2
New Zealand	119	Hamilton 90/91	2	2
Pakistan	116*	Colombo 85/86	1	0
South Africa	27	Moratuwa 93/94	0	0

Coopers & Lybrand world rating (batting): 44 (474)

DESMOND HAYNES

Full name: Desmond Leo Haynes
Born: 15/02/56, Holders Hill, St James, Barbados
Country: West Indies
Right-hand opening batsman - Leg break/googly bowler
Test debut: 03/03/78 v Australia - Queens Park Oval, Port of Spain

Test Career Record: *Batting & Fielding*								
MAT	Inns	N/O	Runs	H/S	Avg	100s	50s	CAT
112	195	24	7270	184	42.51	18	38	65

Test Career Record: *Bowling*							
Balls	Runs	Wkts	Avg	Best	5WI	10WM	BPW
18	8	1	8.00	1-2	0	0	18.00

Overseas tours: Aus 79/80, 81/82, 83/84, 84/85, 86/87, 88/89, 91/92, 92/93, NZ 79/80, 86/87, Eng 80, 84, 88, 91, Pak 80/81, 85/86, 86/87, 90/91, 91/92, Ind 83/84, 87/88, 89/90, 93/94, SA 92/93, SL 93/94, Sharjah 85/86, 86/87, 88/89, 89/90, 93/94, WC: Eng 79, 83, Ind & Pak 86/87, Aus & NZ 91/92, Young WI: Zim 81/82, RW: Eng 87

Test matches: Aus 77/78 (2), Aus 79/80 (3), NZ 79/80 (3), Eng 80 (5), Pak 80/81 (4), Eng 80/81 (4), Aus 81/82 (3), Ind 82/83 (5), Ind 83/84 (6), Aus 83/84 (5), Eng 84 (5), Aus 84/85 (5), NZ 84/85 (4), Eng 85/86 (5), Pak 86/87 (3), NZ 86/87 (3), Ind 87/88 (4), Pak 87/88 (3), Eng 88 (4), Aus 88/89 (5), Ind 88/89 (4), Eng 89/90 (4), Pak 90/91 (3), Aus 90/91 (5), Eng 91 (5), SA 91/92 (1), Aus 92/93 (5), Pak 92/93 (3), SL 93/94 (1)

Highest score against each country:			100s	50s
Australia	145	Bridgetown 83/84	5	14
England	184	Lord's 80	5	12
India	136	St John's 82/83	2	4
New Zealand	122	Christchurch 79/80	3	5
Pakistan	143*	Port of Spain 92/93	3	2
South Africa	58	Bridgetown 91/92	0	1
Sri Lanka	20	Moratuwa 92/93	0	0

Coopers & Lybrand world rating (batting): 2 (818)

IAN HEALY

Full name: Ian Andrew Healy
Born: 30/04/64 Spring Hill, Brisbane, Queensland, Australia
Country: Australia
Right-hand middle order batsman - Wicket-Keeper
Test debut: 15/09/88 v Pakistan - National Stadium, Karachi

Test Career Record: *Batting & Fielding*									
MAT	Inns	N/O	Runs	H/S	Avg	100s	50s	Cat	St
59	86	10	1900	113*	25.00	2	9	186	14

Overseas tours: Pak 88/89, Eng 89, 93, NZ 89/90, 92/93, WI 90/91, SL 92/93, Sharjah 89/90, WC: NZ 91/92

Test matches: Pak 88/89 (3), WI 88/89 (5), Eng 89 (6), NZ 89/90 (1), SL 89/90 (2), Pak 89/90 (3), NZ 89/90 (1), Eng 90/91 (5), WI 90/91 (5), Ind 91/92 (5), SL 92/93 (3), WI 92/93 (5), NZ 92/93 (3), Eng 93 (6), NZ 93/94 (3), SA 93/94 (3)

Highest score against each country:			100s	50s
England	102*	Old Trafford 93	1	3
India	60	Melbourne 91/92	0	1
New Zealand	113*	Perth 93/94	1	1
Pakistan	48	Melbourne 89/90	0	0
South Africa	19	Sydney 93/94	0	0
Sri Lanka	71	Moratuwa 92/93	0	2
West Indies	53	Georgetown 90/91	0	2

Coopers & Lybrand world rating (batting): 49 (437)

GRAEME HICK

Full name: Graeme Ashley Hick
Born: 23/05/66 Salisbury (Harare), Zimbabwe
Country: England
Right-hand middle order batsman - Off break bowler
Test debut: 06/06/91 v West Indies - Headingley, Leeds

Test Career Record: *Batting & Fielding*

MAT	Inns	N/O	Runs	H/S	Avg	100s	50s	Cat
18	31	0	972	178	31.35	1	5	27

Test Career Record: *Bowling*

Balls	Runs	Wkts	Avg	Best	5WI	10WM	BPW
1445	598	14	42.71	4-126	0	0	103.21

Overseas tours: With Zimbabwe: SL 83/84, Eng 85, WC: Eng 83
With England: NZ 91/92, Ind 92/93, SL 92/93, WI 93/94, WC: Aus & NZ 91/92

Test matches: WI 91 (4), NZ 91/92 (3), Pak 92 (4), Ind 92/93 (3), SL 92/93 (1), Aus 93 (3)

Highest score against each country:			100s	50s
Australia	80	The Oval 93	0	2
India	178	Bombay 92/93	1	1
New Zealand	43	Wellington 91/92	0	0
Pakistan	51	Edgbaston 92	0	1
Sri Lanka	68	Colombo 92/93	0	1
West Indies	43	Trent Bridge 91	0	0

Coopers & Lybrand world rating (batting): 31 (554)

CARL HOOPER

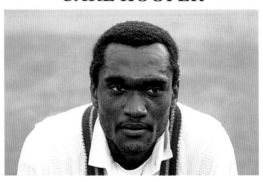

Full name: Carl Llewellyn Hooper
Born: 15/12/66 Georgetown, Guyana
Country: West Indies
Right-hand middle order batsman - Off break bowler
Test debut: 11/12/87 v India - Wankhede Stadium,
Bombay

Test Career Record: *Batting & Fielding*								
MAT	*Inns*	*N/O*	*Runs*	*H/S*	*Avg*	*100s*	*50s*	*Cat*
40	67	6	1832	178*	30.03	4	8	40
Test Career Record: *Bowling*								
Balls	*Runs*	*Wkts*	*Avg*		*Best*	*5WI*	*10WM*	*BPW*
4565	2010	36	55.83		5-40	1	0	126.80

Overseas tours: NZ 86/87, Ind 87/88, 93/94, Eng 88, 91,
Aus 88/89, 91/92, 92/93, Pak 90/91, 91/92, SA 92/93, SL
93/94, Sharjah 88/89, 91/92, 93/94, WC: Ind & Pak 87/
88, Aus & NZ 91/92, Young WI: Zim 86/87, 89/90

Test matches: Ind 87/88 (3), Pak 87/88 (3), Eng 88 (5),
Aus 88/89 (5), Eng 89/90 (3), Pak 90/91 (3), Aus 90/91
(5), Eng 91 (5), Aus 92/93 (4), Pak 92/93 (3), SL 93/94
(1)

Highest score against each country:			100s	50s
Australia	64	Perth 88/89	0	3
England	111	Lord's 91	1	3
India	100*	Calcutta 87/88	1	0
Pakistan	178*	St John's 92/93	2	1
Sri Lanka	62	Moratuwa 92/93	0	1

Coopers & Lybrand world rating (batting): 30 (557)

DAVID HOUGHTON

Full name: David Laud Houghton
Born: 23/06/57 Salisbury (Harare), Zimbabwe
Country: Zimbabwe
Right-hand middle order batsman - Off break bowler
Test debut: 18/10/92 v India - Harare Sports Club

Test Career Record: Batting & Fielding								
MAT	Inns	N/O	Runs	H/S	Avg	100s	50s	Cat
7	12	1	363	121	33.00	1	1	7

Test Career Record: Bowling							
Balls	Runs	Wkts	Avg	Best	5WI	10WM	BPW
5	0	0	-	-	-	-	-

Overseas tours: Eng 82, 85, 93, SL 83/84, Ind 92/93, 93/94, Pak 93/94, Sharjah 92/93, WC: Eng 83, Ind 87/88, Aus & NZ 91/92

Test matches: Ind 92/93 (1), NZ 92/93 (2), Ind 92/93 (1), Pak 93/94 (3)

Highest score against each country:			100s	50s
India	121	Harare 92/93	1	0
New Zealand	36	Bulawayo 92/93	0	0
Pakistan	50	Lahore 93/94	0	1

Coopers & Lybrand world rating (batting): 71 (323)*

ANDREW HUDSON

Full name: Andrew Charles Hudson
Born: 17/03/66 Eshowe, Zululand, South Africa
Country: South Africa
Right-hand middle order batsman - Right-arm medium bowler
Test debut: 18/04/92 v West Indies, Kensington Oval, Bridgetown

Test Career Record: *Batting & Fielding*

MAT	Inns	N/O	Runs	H/S	Avg	100s	50s	Cat
11	20	1	767	163	40.36	1	7	9

Overseas tours: Ind 91/92, 93/94, WI 91/92, SL 93/94, Aus 93/94, WC: Aus & NZ 91/92

Test matches: WI 91/92 (1), Ind 92/93 (4), SL 93/94 (3), Aus 93/94 (3)

Highest score against each current:			100s	50s
Australia	90	Adelaide 93/94	0	2
India	55	Durban 92/93	0	3
Sri Lanka	90	Moratuwa 93/94	0	2
West Indies	163	Bridgetown 91/92	1	0

Coopers & Lybrand world rating (batting): 17 (604)

MERV HUGHES

Full name: Mervyn Gregory Hughes
Born: 23/11/61 Euroa, Victoria, Australia
Country: Australia
Right arm fast medium bowler - Right-hand lower order batsman
Test debut: 13/12/85 v India - Adelaide Oval

Test Career Record: *Batting & Fielding*

MAT	Inns	N/O	Runs	H/S	Avg	100s	50s	Cat
51	67	7	999	72*	16.65	0	2	22

Test Career Record: *Bowling*

Balls	Runs	Wkts	Avg	Best	5WI	10WM	BPW
11865	5780	208	27.78	8-87	7	1	57.04

Overseas tours: Eng 89, 93, Ind 89/90, NZ 89/90, 92/93, WI 90/91 Sharjah: 89/90

Test matches: Ind 85/86 (1), Eng 86/87 (4), NZ 87/88 (1), SL 87/88 (1), WI 88/89 (4), Eng 89 (6), NZ 89/90 (1), SL 89/90 (2), Pak 89/90 (3), Eng 90/91 (4), WI 90/91 (5), Ind 91/92 (5), WI 92/93 (5), NZ 92/93 (3), Eng 93 (6)

Best bowling against each country:			5WI	10WM
England	5-92	Trent Bridge 93	1	0
India	4-50	Brisbane 91/92	0	0
New Zealand	4-51	Perth 89/90	0	0
Pakistan	5-111	Sydney 89/90	1	0
Sri Lanka	5-67	Perth 87/88	2	0
West Indies	8-87	Perth 88/89	3	1

Coopers & Lybrand world rating (bowling): 9 (683)

NASSER HUSSAIN

Full name: Nasser Hussain
Born: 28/03/68 Madras, India
Country: England
Right-hand middle order batsman - Occasional leg break bowler
Test debut: 24/02/90 v West Indies - Sabina Park, Kingston

Test Career Record: *Batting & Fielding*								
MAT	Inns	N/O	Runs	H/S	Avg	100s	50s	Cat
7	13	2	284	71	25.81	0	1	3

Overseas tours: Ind 89/90, WI 89/90, 93/94, Eng A: Pak & SL 90/91, WI 91/92

Test matches: WI 89/90 (3), Aus 93 (4)

Highest score against each country:			100s	50s
Australia	71	Trent Bridge 93	0	1
West Indies	35	St John's 89/90	0	0

Coopers & Lybrand world rating (batting): 75 (271)*

INZAMAM-UL-HAQ

Full name: Inzamam-ul-Haq
Born: 03/03/70 Multan, Pakistan
Country: Pakistan
Right-hand middle order batsman - Left-arm slow bowler
Test debut: 04/06/92 v England - Edgbaston, Birmingham

Test Career Record: Batting & Fielding

MAT	Inns	N/O	Runs	H/S	Avg	100s	50s	Cat
14	23	4	722	135*	38.00	2	2	16

Overseas tours: Aus 91/92, 92/93, Eng 92, NZ 92/93, 93/94, WI 92/93, SA 92/93, Sharjah 92/93, 93/94, WC: Aus & NZ 91/92, Pak A: SL 90/91

Test matches: Eng 92 (4), NZ 92/93 (1), WI 92/93 (3), Zim 93/94 (3), NZ 93/94 (3)

Highest score against each country:			100s	50s
England	26	Old Trafford 92	0	0
New Zealand	135*	Wellington 93/94	1	1
West Indies	123	St John's 92/93	1	0
Zimbabwe	57*	Karachi 93/94	0	1

Coopers & Lybrand world rating (batting): 45 (472)*

JAVED MIANDAD

Full name: Javed Miandad Khan
Born: 12/06/57 Karachi, Pakistan
Country: Pakistan
Right-hand middle order batsman   Leg break & googly
bowler
Test debut: 09/10/76 v New Zealand - Gaddafi Stadium,
Lahore

Test Career Record: *Batting & Fielding*

MAT	Inns	N/O	Runs	H/S	Avg	100s	50s	Cat	St
124	189	21	8832	280*	52.57	23	43	93	1

Test Career Record: *Bowling*

Balls	Runs	Wkts	Avg	Best	5WI	10WM	BPW
1470	682	17	40.11	3-74	0	0	86.47

Overseas tours: SL 75/76, 85/86, Aus 76/77, 78/79, 81/
82, 83/84, 84/85, 86/87, 88/89, 89/90, 92/93, WI 76/77,
87/88, 92/93, Eng 78, 82, 87, 92, NZ 78/79, 84/85, 88/89,
92/93, Ind 79/80, 83/84, 86/87, 89/90, Ban 88/89, S/A 92/
93, Zim 92/93, Sharjah 83/84, 84/85, 85/86, 86/87, 88/89,
89/90, 90/91, 91/92, 92/93, 93/94, WC: Eng 75, 79, 83,
Aus & NZ 91/92, RW: Eng 87

Test matches: NZ 76/77 (3), Aus 76/77 (3), WI 76/77
(1), Eng 77/78 (3), Eng 78 (3), Ind 78/79 (3), NZ 78/79
(3), Aus 78/79 (2), Ind 79/80 (6), Aus 79/80 (3), WI 80/81
(4), Aus 81/82 (3), SL 81/82 (3), Eng 82 (3), Aus 82/83
(3), Ind 82/83 (6), Ind 83/84 (3), Aus 83/84 (5), Ind 84/85
(2), NZ 84/85 (3), NZ 84/85 (3), SL 85/86 (3), SL 85/86
(3), WI 86/87 (3), Ind 86/87 (4), Eng 87 (5), Eng 87/88
(3), WI 87/88 (3), Aus 88/89 (3), NZ 88/89 (2), Ind 89/90
(4), Aus 89/90 (3), NZ 90/91 (3), WI 90/91 (2), SL 91/92

(3), Eng 92 (5), NZ 92/93 (1), WI 92/93 (3), Zim 93/94 (3)

Highest score against each country:			100s	50s
Australia	211	Karachi 88/89	6	7
England	260	The Oval 87	2	9
India	280*	Hyderabad 82/83	5	14
New Zealand	271	Auckland 88/89	7	6
Sri Lanka	203*	Faisalabad 85/86	1	2
West Indies	114	Georgetown 87/88	2	4
Zimbabwe	70	Karachi 93/94	0	1

Coopers & Lybrand world rating (batting): 19 (599)

SANATH JAYASURIYA

Full name: Sanath Teran Jayasuriya
Born: 30/06/69 Matara, Sri Lanka
Country: Sri Lanka
Left-hand middle order batsman - Left-arm slow bowler
Test debut: 22/02/91 v New Zealand - Trust Bank Park, Hamilton

Test Career Record: *Batting & Fielding*

MAT	Inns	N/O	Runs	H/S	Avg	100s	50s	Cat
14	22	5	591	81	34.76	0	4	14

Test Career Record: *Bowling*

Balls	Runs	Wkts	Avg	Best	5WI	10WM	BPW
480	280	4	70.00	2-46	0	0	120.00

Overseas tours: Aus 89/90, Ind 89/90, 90/91, 93/94, Eng 90, 91, NZ 90/91, Pak 91/92, Sharjah 90/91, 93/94, WC: Aus & NZ 91/92, SL B: Pak 88/89

Test matches: NZ 90/91 (2), Eng 91 (1), Pak 91/92 (3), Aus 92/93 (2), Eng 92/93 (1), Ind 93/94 (1), SA 93/94 (2), WI 93/94 (1), Ind 93/94 (1)

Highest score against each country:			100s	50s
Australia	19	Colombo 92/93	0	0
England	66	Lord's 91	0	1
India	31*	Colombo 93/94	0	0
New Zealand	35	Hamilton 90/91	0	0
Pakistan	81	Faisalabad 91/92	0	2
South Africa	65	Colombo 93/94	0	1
West Indies	0	Moratuwa 93/94	0	0

Coopers & Lybrand world rating (batting): 36 (515)

ANDREW JONES

Full name: Andrew Howard Jones
Born: 09/05/59 Wellington, New Zealand
Country: New Zealand
Right-hand middle order batsman   Off break bowler
Test Debut: 16/04/87 v Sri Lanka - Colombo Cricket Club Ground

Test Career Record: *Batting & Fielding*

MAT	Inns	N/O	Runs	H/S	Avg	100s	50s	Cat
37	70	7	2898	186	46.00	7	11	24

Test Career Record: *Bowling*

Balls	Runs	Wkts	Avg	Best	5WI	10WM	BPW
244	139	1	139.00	1-40	0	0	244.00

Overseas tours: SL 86/87, 92/93, Aus 87/88, 89/90, 90/91, 93/94, Ind 88/89, Eng 90, Zim 92/93, Sharjah 87/88, 89/90, WC: Ind 87/88

Test matches: SL 86/87 (1), Aus 87/88 (3), Eng 87/88 (1), Ind 88/89 (3), Pak 88/89 (2), Ind 89/90 (3), Aus 89/90 (1), Eng 90 (3), SL 90/91 (3), Eng 91/92 (3), Zim 92/93 (2), SL 92/93 (2), Pak 92/93 (1), Aus 92/93 (3), Aus 93/94 (3), Pak 93/94 (3)

Highest score against each country:			100s	50s
Australia	150	Adelaide 87/88	2	2
England	143	Wellington 91/92	1	1
India	170	Auckland 89/90	1	2
Pakistan	86	Wellington	0	4
Sri Lanka	186	Wellington 90/91	3	1
Zimbabwe	67*	Bulawayo 92/93	0	1

Coopers & Lybrand world rating (batting): 32= (549)

DEAN JONES

Full name: Dean Mervyn Jones
Born: 24/03/61 Coburg, Melbourne, Victoria, Australia
Country: Australia
Right-hand middle order batsman - Right-arm medium
bowler
Test debut: 16/03/84 v West Indies - Queens Park Oval,
Port of Spain

Test Career Record: *Batting & Fielding*

MAT	Inns	N/O	Runs	H/S	Avg	100s	50s	Cat
52	89	11	3631	216	46.55	11	14	34

Test Career Record: *Bowling*

Balls	Runs	Wkts	Avg	Best	5WI	10WM	BPW
198	64	1	64.00	1-5	0	0	198.00

Overseas tours: WI 83/84, 90/91, Ind 86/87, 89/90, Pak
88/89, Eng 89, NZ 89/90, Sharjah 84/85, 85/86, 89/90,
WC: Ind & Pak 87/88, NZ 91/92, Young Aus: Zim 85/86,
RW: Eng 87
Test matches: WI 83/84 (2), Ind 86/87 (3), Eng 86/87
(5), NZ 87/88 (3), Eng 87/88 (1), SL 87/88 (1), Pak 88/89
(3), WI 88/89 (3), Eng 89 (6), NZ 89/90 (1), SL 89/90 (2),
Pak 89/90 (3), NZ 89/90 (1), Eng 90/91 (5), WI 90/91 (5),
Ind 91/92 (5), SL 92/93 (3),

Highest score against each country:			100s	50s
England	184*	Sydney 86/87	3	8
India	210	Madras 86/87	2	2
New Zealand	99	Perth 89/90	0	1
Pakistan	121*	Adelaide 89/90	2	0
Sri Lanka	118*	Hobart 89/90	3	2
West Indies	216	Adelaide 88/89	1	1

Coopers & Lybrand world rating (batting): 35 (525)

VINOD KAMBLI

Full name: Vinod Ganpat Kambli
Born: 18/01/72 Bombay, India
Country: India
Left-hand middle order batsman   Off break bowler
Test debut: 29/01/93 v England - Eden Gardens, Calcutta

Test Career Record: *Batting & Fielding*								
MAT	*Inns*	*N/O*	*Runs*	*H/S*	*Avg*	*100s*	*50s*	*Cat*
10	11	1	937	227	93.70	4	3	4

Overseas tours: SA 92/93, SL 93/94, Sharjah 91/92

Test matches: Eng 92/93 (3), Zim 92/93 (1), SL 93/94 (3), SL 93/94 (3)

Highest score against each country:			100s	50s
England	224	Bombay 92/93	1	1
Sri Lanka	125	Colombo 93/94	2	2
Zimbabwe	227	Delhi 92/93	1	0

Coopers & Lybrand world rating (batting): 9 (673)*

KAPIL DEV

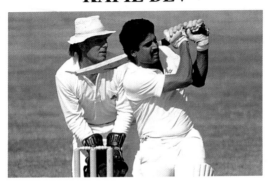

Full name: Kapil Dev Ramlal Nikhanj
Born: 06/01/59 Chandigarh, India
Country: India
Right-arm fast medium bowler - Right-hand middle order
batsman
Test debut: 16/10/78 v Pakistan - Iqbal Stadium,
Faisalabad

Test Career Record: *Batting & Fielding*

MAT	Inns	N/O	Runs	H/S	Avg	100s	50s	Cat
130	183	15	5230	163	31.13	8	27	63

Test Career Record: *Bowling*

Balls	Runs	Wkts	Avg	Best	5WI	10WM	BPW
27590	12795	432	29.61	9-83	23	2	63.86

Overseas tours: Pak 78/79, 82/83, 84/85, 89/90, Eng 79,
82, 86, 90, Aus 80/81, 84/85, 85/86, 91/92, NZ 80/81, 89/
90, WI 82/83, 88/89, SL 85/86, 93/94, Zim 92/93, SA 92/
93, Ban 88/89, Sharjah 84/85, 85/86, 86/87, 87/88, 88/89,
89/90, 91/92, WC: Eng 79, 83, Aus & NZ 91/92, RW:
Eng 87, 91

Test matches: Pak 78/79 (3), WI 78/79 (6), Eng 79 (4),
Aus 79/80 (6), Pak 79/80 (6), Eng 79/80 (1), Aus 80/81
(3), NZ 80/81 (3), Eng 81/82 (6), Eng 82 (3), SL 82/83
(1), Pak 82/83 (6), WI 82/83 (5), Pak 83/84 (3), WI 83/84
(6), Pak 84/85 (2), Eng 84/85 (4), SL 85/86 (3), Aus 85/86
(3), Eng 86 (3), Aus 86/87 (3), SL 86/87 (3), Pak 86/87
(5), WI 87/88 (4), NZ 88/89 (3), WI 88/89 (4), Pak 89/90
(4), NZ 89/90 (3), Eng 90 (3), SL 90/91 (1), Aus 91/92
(5), Zim 92/93 (1), S/A 92/93 (4), Eng 92/93 (3), Zim 92/
93 (1), SL 93/94 (3), SL 93/94 (3)

Best bowling against each country:			5WI	10WM
Australia	8-106	Adelaide 85/86	7	0
England	6-91	Calcutta 81/82	4	0
New Zealand	4-34	Wellington 80/81	0	0
Pakistan	8-85	Lahore 82/83	7	1
South Africa	3-43	Durban 92/93	0	0
Sri Lanka	5-110	Madras 82/83	1	0
West Indies	9-83	Ahmedabad 83/84	4	1
Zimbabwe	2-22	Harare 92/93	0	0

Coopers & Lybrand world rating (bowling): 14 (605)

ANIL KUMBLE

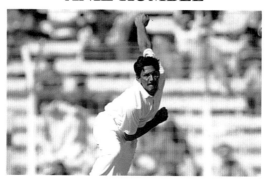

Full name: Anil Radhakrishna Kumble
Born: 17/10/70 Bangalore, India
Country: India
Leg break & googly bowler - Right-hand lower order
batsman
Test debut: 09/08/90 v England - Old Trafford, Manchester

Test Career Record: *Batting & Fielding*

MAT	Inns	N/O	Runs	H/S	Avg	100s	50s	Cat
16	14	2	125	21*	10.41	0	0	7

Test Career Record: *Bowling*

Balls	Runs	Wkts	Avg	Best	5WI	10WM	BPW
5392	1999	84	23.79	7-59	5	1	64.19

Overseas tours: Eng 90, Zim 92/93, SA 92/93, SL 93/94,
Sharjah 89/90, 91/92

Test matches: Eng 90 (1), Zim 92/93 (1), SA 92/93 (4),
Eng 92/93 (3), Zim 92/93 (1), SL 93/94 (3), SL 93/94 (3)

Best bowling against each country:			5WI	10WM
England	6-64	Madras 92/93	1	0
South Africa	6-53	Johannesburg 92/93	1	0
Sri Lanka	7-59	Lucknow 93/94	2	1
Zimbabwe	5-70	Delhi 92/93	1	0

Coopers & Lybrand world rating (bowling): 2 (890)

BRIAN LARA

Full name: Brian Charles Lara
Born: 02/05/69 Santa Cruz, Trinidad
Country: West Indies
Left-hand middle order batsman - Leg break & googly
bowler
Test debut: 06/12/90 v Pakistan - Gaddafi Stadium,
Lahore

Test Career Record: *Batting & Fielding*								
MAT	Inns	N/O	Runs	H/S	Avg	100s	50s	Cat
11	18	0	830	277	46.11	1	6	18

Test Career Record: *Bowling*							
Balls	Runs	Wkts	Avg	Best	5WI	10WM	BPW
12	4	0	-	-	-	-	-

Overseas tours: Pak 90/91, 91/92, Eng 91, Aus 91/92,
92/93, SA 92/93, Ind 93/94, SL 93/94, Sharjah 91/92, 93/
94 WC: Aus & NZ 91/92, Young WI: Zim 89/90

Test matches: Pak 90/91 (1), SA 91/92 (1), Aus 92/93
(5), Pak 92/93 (3), SL 93/94 (1)

Highest score against each country:			100s	50s
Australia	277	Sydney 92/93	1	3
Pakistan	96	Port of Spain 92/93	0	2
South Africa	64	Bridgetown 91/92	0	1
Sri Lanka	18	Moratuwa 93/94	0	0

Coopers & Lybrand world rating (batting): 6 (696)*

CHRIS LEWIS

Full name: Clairmonte Christopher Lewis
Born: 14/02/68 Georgetown, Guyana
Country: England
Right-arm fast medium bowler - Right-hand middle order batsman
Test debut: 05/07/90 v New Zealand - Edgbaston, Birmingham

Test Career Record: *Batting & Fielding*

MAT	Inns	N/O	Runs	H/S	Avg	100s	50s	Cat
20	31	1	771	117	25.70	1	3	18

Test Career Record: *Bowling*

Balls	Runs	Wkts	Avg	Best	5WI	10WM	BPW
4152	2068	52	39.76	6-111	2	0	79.84

Overseas tours: WI 89/90, 93/94, Aus 90/91, NZ 91/92, Ind 92/93, SL 92/93, WC: Aus & NZ 91/92, Eng A: Zim 89/90

Test matches: NZ 90 (1), Ind 90 (2), Aus 90/91 (1), WI 91 (2), SL 91 (1), NZ 91/92 (2), Pak 92 (5), Ind 92/93 (3), SL 92/93 (1), Aus 93 (2)

Best bowling against each country:			5WI	10WM
Australia	3-29	Brisbane 90/91	0	0
India	2-26	Lord's 90	0	0
New Zealand	5-31	Auckland 91/92	1	0
Pakistan	3-43	Lord's 92	0	0
Sri Lanka	4-66	Colombo 92/93	0	0
West Indies	6-111	Edgbaston 91	1	0

Coopers & Lybrand world rating (bowling): 29 (381)

ROSHAN MAHANAMA

Full name: Roshan Siriwardene Mahanama
Born: 31/05/66 Colombo, Sri Lanka
Country: Sri Lanka
Right-hand opening batsman
Test debut: 14/03/86 v Pakistan - P. Saravanamuttu
Stadium, Colombo

Test Career Record: *Batting & Fielding*

MAT	Inns	N/O	Runs	H/S	Avg	100s	50s	Cat
27	44	0	1580	153	35.90	3	9	17

Test Career Record: *Bowling*

Balls	Runs	Wkts	Avg	Best	5WI	10WM	BPW
36	30	0	-	-	-	-	-

Overseas tours: Ind 86/87, 89/90, 90/91, 93/94, Aus 87/
88, 89/90, Eng 88, 90, 91, NZ 90/91, Pak 91/92, Ban 88/
89, Sharjah 85/86, 86/87, 87/88, 88/89, 90/91, 92/93, 93/
94, WC: Ind & Pak 87/88, Aus & NZ 91/92
Test matches: Pak 85/86 (2), NZ 86/87 (1), Aus 87/88
(1), Aus 89/90 (2), Ind 90/91 (1), NZ 90/91 (1), Eng 91
(1), Pak 91/92 (2), Aus 92/93 (3), NZ 92/93 (2), Eng 92/
93 (1), Ind 93/94 (3), SA 93/94 (3), WI 93/94 (1), Ind 93/
94 (3)

Highest score against each country:			100s	50s
Australia	85	Hobart 89/90	0	4
England	64	Colombo 92/93	0	1
India	151	Colombo 93/94	1	2
New Zealand	153	Moratuwa 92/93	2	0
Pakistan	58	Faisalabad 91/92	0	1
South Africa	53	Moratuwa 93/94	0	1
West Indies	11	Moratuwa 93/94	0	0

Coopers & Lybrand world rating (batting): 23 (589)

DEVON MALCOLM

Full name: Devon Eugene Malcolm
Born: 22/02/63 Kingston, Jamaica
Country: England
Right-arm fast bowler - Right-hand lower order batsman
Test debut: 10/08/89 v Australia - Trent Bridge,
Nottingham

Test Career Record: *Batting & Fielding*								
MAT	Inns	N/O	Runs	H/S	Avg	100s	50s	Cat
25	37	13	130	15*	5.41	0	0	3

Test Career Record: *Bowling*							
Balls	Runs	Wkts	Avg	Best	5WI	10WM	BPW
5607	3084	83	37.15	6-77	4	1	67.55

Overseas tours: WI 89/90, 93/94, Aus 90/91, Ind 92/93,
SL 92/93, Eng A: WI 91/92

Test matches: Aus 89 (1), WI 89/90 (4), NZ 90 (3), Ind
90 (3), Aus 90/91 (5), WI 91 (2), Pak 92 (3), Ind 92/93
(2), SL 92/93 (1), Aus 93 (1)

Best bowling against each country:			5WI	10WM
Australia	4-128	Sydney 90/91	0	0
India	3-67	Calcutta 92/93	0	0
New Zealand	5-46	Edgbaston 90	2	0
Pakistan	5-94	The Oval 92	1	0
Sri Lanka	0-11	Colombo 92/93	0	0
West Indies	6-77	Port of Spain 89/90	1	1

Coopers & Lybrand world rating (bowling): 25 (128)

MANINDER SINGH

Full name: Maninder Singh
Born: 13/06/65 Poona, India
Country: India
Left-arm slow bowler - Right-hand lower order batsman
Test debut: 23/12/82 v Pakistan - National Stadium, Karachi

Test Career Record: *Batting & Fielding*								
MAT	Inns	N/O	Runs	H/S	Avg	100s	50s	Cat
35	38	12	99	15	3.80	0	0	9
Test Career Record: *Bowling*							
Balls	Runs	Wkts	Avg	Best	5WI	10WM	BPW
8218	3288	88	37.36	7-27	3	2	93.38

Overseas tours: WI 82/83, Pak 82/83, 84/85, 89/90, SL 85/86, Eng 86, Ban 88/89, Sharjah 85/86, 86/87, 88/89, Young Ind: Zim 83/84, RW: Eng 87, 88, 89, 91

Test matches: Pak 82/83 (5), WI 82/83 (3), WI 83/84 (4), Ind 84/85 (1), SL 85/86 (2), Eng 86 (3), Aus 86/87 (3), SL 86/87 (3), Pak 86/87 (4), WI 87/88 (3), Pak 89/90 (3), Zim 92/93 (1)

Best bowling against each country:			5WI	10WM
Australia	3-60	Madras 86/87	0	0
England	4-26	Headingley 86	0	0
Pakistan	7-27	Bangalore 86/87	2	1
Sri Lanka	7-51	Nagpur 86/87	1	1
West Indies	4-85	Ahmedabad 83/84	0	0
Zimbabwe	4-66	Delhi 92/93	0	0

Coopers & Lybrand world rating (bowling): 31 (362)

SANJAY MANJREKAR

Full name: Sanjay Vijay Manjrekar
Born: 12/07/65 Mangalore, India
Country: India
Right-hand middle order batsman • Off break bowler
Test debut: 25/11/87 v West Indies - Feroz Kotla, Delhi

Test Career Record: *Batting & Fielding*

MAT	Inns	N/O	Runs	H/S	Avg	100s	50s	Cat
29	45	4	1639	218	39.97	4	6	17

Test Career Record: *Bowling*

Balls	Runs	Wkts	Avg	Best	5WI	10WM	BPW
17	15	0	-	-	-	-	-

Overseas tours: WI 88/89, Pak 89/90, NZ 89/90, Eng 90, Aus 91/92, Zim 92/93, SA 92/93, Sharjah 89/90, 91/92, WC: Aus & NZ 91/92, RW: Eng 91

Test matches: WI 87/88 (1), WI 88/89 (4), Pak 89/90 (4), NZ 89/90 (3), Eng 90 (3), SL 90/91 (1), Aus 91/92 (5), Zim 92/93 (1), SA 92/93 (4), SL 93/94 (3)

Highest score against each country:			100s	50s
England	93	Old Trafford 90	0	2
New Zealand	42	Napier 89/90	0	0
Pakistan	218	Lahore 89/90	2	3
South Africa	46	Cape Town 92/93	0	0
Sri Lanka	61	Lucknow 93/94	0	1
West Indies	108	Bridgetown 88/89	1	0
Zimbabwe	104	Harare 92/93	1	0

Coopers & Lybrand world rating (batting): 40= (486)

DAMIEN MARTYN

Full name: Damien Richard Martyn
Born: 21/10/71 Darwin, Northern Territories, Australia
Country: Australia
Right-hand middle order batsman - Right-arm medium bowler
Test debut: 27/11/92 v West Indies - Woolloongabba, Brisbane

Test Career Record: *Batting & Fielding*

MAT	Inns	N/O	Runs	H/S	Avg	100s	50s	Cat
7	12	1	317	74	28.81	0	3	1

Test Career Record: *Bowling*

Balls	Runs	Wkts	Avg	Best	5WI	10WM	BPW
6	0	0	-	-	-	-	-

Overseas tours: SL 92/93, NZ 92/93, Eng 93, Aus under 19: Eng 91

Test matches: WI 92/93 (4), NZ 92/93 (1), SA 93/94 (2)

Highest score against each country:			100s	50s
New Zealand	74	Auckland 92/93	0	1
South Africa	59	Sydney 93/94	0	1
West Indies	67*	Melbourne 92/93	0	1

Coopers & Lybrand world rating (batting): 56 (386)*

TIM MAY

Full name: Timothy Brian Alexander May
Born: 26/01/62 North Adelaide, South Australia
Country: Australia
Off break bowler - Right-hand lower order batsman
Test debut: 11/12/87 v New Zealand - Adelaide Oval

Test Career Record: *Batting & Fielding*

MAT	Inns	N/O	Runs	H/S	Avg	100s	50s	Cat
18	18	8	169	42*	16.90	0	0	6

Test Career Record: *Bowling*

Balls	Runs	Wkts	Avg	Best	5WI	10WM	BPW
5053	1967	64	30.73	5-9	3	0	78.95

Overseas tours: Pak 88/89, Eng 89, 93, Ind 89/90, NZ 92/93, WC: Ind & Pak 87/88

Test matches: NZ 87/88 (1), Pak 88/89 (3), WI 88/89 (3), WI 92/93 (1), Eng 93 (5), NZ 93/94 (2), SA 93/94 (3)

Best bowling against each country:			5WI	10WM
England	5-89	Edgbaston 93	1	0
New Zealand	5-65	Hobart 93/94	1	0
Pakistan	4-97	Karachi 88/89	0	0
South Africa	2-26	Adelaide 93/94	0	0
West Indies	5-9	Adelaide 92/93	1	0

Coopers & Lybrand world rating (bowling): 19 (548)

CRAIG MCDERMOTT

Full name: Craig John McDermott
Born: 14/04/65 Ipswich, Queensland, Australia
Country: Australia
Right-arm fast bowler - Right-hand lower order batsman
Test debut: 22/12/84 v West Indies - Melbourne Cricket
Ground

Test Career Record: *Batting & Fielding*

MAT	Inns	N/O	Runs	H/S	Avg	100s	50s	Cat
55	70	9	769	42*	12.60	0	0	11

Test Career Record: *Bowling*

Balls	Runs	Wkts	Avg	Best	5WI	10WM	BPW
12630	6324	224	28.23	8-97	9	2	56.38

Overseas tours: Eng 85, 93, NZ 85/86, 92/93, Ind 86/87,
Pak 89/90, WI 90/91, SL 92/93, Sharjah 84/85, 85/86,
WC: Ind & Pak 87/88, NZ 91/92

Test matches: WI 84/85 (2), Eng 85 (6), NZ 85/86 (2),
Ind 85/86 (2), NZ 85/86 (2), Ind 86/87 (2), Eng 86/87 (1),
NZ 87/88 (3), Eng 87/88 (1), SL 87/88 (1), WI 88/89 (2),
Eng 90/91 (2), WI 90/91 (5), Ind 91/92 (5), SL 92/93 (3),
WI 92/93 (5), NZ 92/93 (3), Eng 93 (2), NZ 93/94 (3), SA
93/94 (3)

Best bowling against each country:			5WI	10WM
England	8-97	Perth 90/91	4	1
India	5-54	Brisbane 91/92	3	1
New Zealand	5-97	Melbourne 87/88	1	0
South Africa	4-33	Adelaide 93/94	0	0
Sri Lanka	4-53	Colombo 92/93	0	0
West Indies	5-80	Kingston 90/91	1	0

Coopers & Lybrand world rating (bowling): 7 (701)

BRIAN MCMILLAN

Full name: Brian Mervin McMillan
Born: 22/12/63 Welkom, South Africa
Country: South Africa
Right-arm medium fast bowler - Right-hand middle order batsman
Test debut: 13/11/92 v India - Kingsmead, Durban, South Africa

Test Career Record: *Batting & Fielding*

MAT	Inns	N/O	Runs	H/S	Avg	100s	50s	Cat
7	11	2	202	98	22.44	0	2	10

Test Career Record: *Bowling*

Balls	Runs	Wkts	Avg	Best	5WI	10WM	BPW
1434	542	19	28.52	4-74	0	0	75.47

Overseas tours: Ind 91/92, 93/94, SL 93/94, Aus 93/94, WC: Aus & NZ 91/92

Test matches: Ind 92/93 (4), SL 93/94 (2), Aus 93/94 (1)

Best bowling against each country:			5WI	10WM
Australia	3-89	Adelaide 93/94	0	0
India	4-74	Johannesburg 92/93	0	0
Sri Lanka	1-11	Colombo 93/94	0	0

Coopers & Lybrand world rating (bowling): 43 (297)*

KIRAN MORE

Full name: Kiran Shankar More
Born: 04/09/62 Baroda, India
Country: India
Right-hand middle order batsman - Wicket-Keeper
Test debut: 05/06/86 v England - Lord's, London

Test Career Record: *Batting & Fielding*

MAT	Inns	N/O	Runs	H/S	Avg	100s	50s	Cat	St
49	64	14	1285	73	25.70	0	7	110	20

Test Career Record: *Bowling*

Balls	Runs	Wkts	Avg	Best	5WI	10WM	BPW
12	12	0	-	-	-	-	-

Overseas tours: WI 82/83, 88/89, Aus 85/86, 91/92, Eng 86, 90, Pak 89/90, NZ 89/90, Ban 88/89, Sharjah 87/88, 88/89, 89/90, 91/92, WC: Aus & NZ 91/92
Test matches: Eng 86 (3), Aus 86/87 (2), SL 86/87 (3), Pak 86/87 (5), WI 87/88 (4), NZ 88/89 (3), WI 88/89 (4), Pak 89/90 (4), NZ 89/90 (3), Eng 90 (3), SL 90/91 (1), Aus 91/92 (3), Zim 92/93 (1), SA 92/93 (4), Eng 92/93 (3), SL 93/94 (3)

Highest score against each country:			100s	50s
Australia	67*	Melbourne 91/92	0	1
England	61*	The Oval 90	0	1
New Zealand	73	Napier 89/90	0	2
Pakistan	58*	Karachi 89/90	0	1
South Africa	55	Durban 92/93	0	1
Sri Lanka	37*	Chandigarh 90/91	0	0
West Indies	50	Bridgetown 88/89	0	1
Zimbabwe	41	Harare 92/93	0	0

Coopers & Lybrand world rating (batting): 65= (343)

DANNY MORRISON

Full name: Daniel Kyle Morrison
Born: 03/02/66 Auckland, New Zealand
Country: New Zealand
Right-arm fast medium bowler - Right-hand lower order batsman
Test debut: 04/12/87 v Australia - Woolloongabba, Brisbane

Test Career Record: *Batting & Fielding*

MAT	Inns	N/O	Runs	H/S	Avg	100s	50s	Cat
34	50	16	257	42	7.55	0	0	13

Test Career Record: *Bowling*

Balls	Runs	Wkts	Avg	Best	5WI	10WM	BPW
7304	4114	116	35.46	7-89	8	0	62.96

Overseas tours: SL 86/87, 92/93, Aus 87/88, 89/90, 90/91, 93/94, Ind 88/89, Eng 90, Pak 90/91, Zim 92/93, Sharjah 87/88, 89/90, WC: Ind 87/88, Young NZ: Zim 88/89, RW: Eng 91

Test matches: Aus 87/88 (3), Eng 87/88 (3), Ind 88/89 (1), Pak 88/89 (1), Aus 89/90 (1), Ind 89/90 (3), Aus 89/90 (1), Eng 90 (3), Pak 90/91 (3), SL 90/91 (3), Eng 91/92 (3), Pak 92/93 (1), Aus 92/93 (3), Aus 93/94 (3), Pak 93/94 (2)

Best bowling against each country:			5WI	10WM
Australia	7-89	Wellington 92/93	2	0
England	5-69	Christchurch 87/88	1	0
India	5-75	Christchurch 89/90	3	0
Pakistan	5-41	Hamilton 92/93	1	0
Sri Lanka	5-153	Wellington 90/91	1	0

Coopers & Lybrand world rating (bowling): 21 (493)

MUTTIAH MURALITHARAN

Full name: Muttiah Muralitharan
Born: 17/04/72 Kandy, Sri Lanka
Country: Sri Lanka
Right-hand lower order batsman - Off break bowler
Test debut: 28/08/92 v Australia - Khettarama Stadium, Colombo

Test Career Record: *Batting & Fielding*

MAT	Inns	N/O	Runs	H/S	Avg	100s	50s	Cat
13	14	9	93	20*	18.60	0	0	5

Test Career Record: *Bowling*

Balls	Runs	Wkts	Avg	Best	5WI	10WM	BPW
3396	1513	52	29.09	5-101	3	0	65.30

Overseas tours: Eng 91, Ind 93/94, Sharjah 93/94

Test matches: Aus 92/93 (2), NZ 92/93 (1), Eng 92/93 (1), Ind 93/94 (2), SA 93/94 (3), WI 93/94 (1), Ind 93/94 (3)

Best bowling against each country:		5WI	10WM
Australia	2-109 Colombo 92/93	0	0
England	4-118 Colombo 92/93	0	0
India	5-162 Lucknow 93/94	1	0
New Zealand	4-134 Colombo 92/93	0	0
South Africa	5-101 Colombo 93/94	2	0
West Indies	4-47 Moratuwa 93/94	0	0

Coopers & Lybrand world rating (bowling): 12 (643)

JUNIOR MURRAY

Full name: Junior Randalph Murray
Born: 20/01/68 St George's, Grenada
Country: West Indies
Right-hand middle order batsman - Wicket-Keeper
Test debut: 02/01/93 v Australia - Sydney Cricket
Ground

Test Career Record: *Batting & Fielding*

MAT	Inns	N/O	Runs	H/S	Avg	100s	50s	Cat	St
7	9	1	143	49*	17.87	0	0	29	1

Overseas tours: Aus 92/93, SA 92/93, Ind 93/94, SL 93/94, Sharjah 93/94

Test matches: Aus 92/93 (3), Pak 92/93 (3), SL 93/94 (1)

Highest score against each country:			100s	50s
Australia	49*	Adelaide 92/93	0	0
Pakistan	35	Bridgetown 92/93	0	0
Sri Lanka	7	Moratuwa 93/94	0	0

Coopers & Lybrand world rating (batting): 86 (218)*

MUSHTAQ AHMED

Full name: Mushtaq Ahmed
Born: 28/06/70 Sahiwal, Pakistan
Country: Pakistan
Leg break & googly bowler - Right-hand lower order batsman
Test debut: 19/01/90 v Australia - Adelaide Oval

Test Career Record: *Batting & Fielding*

MAT	Inns	N/O	Runs	H/S	Avg	100s	50s	Cat
13	18	3	95	18	6.33	0	0	3

Test Career Record: *Bowling*

Balls	Runs	Wkts	Avg	Best	5WI	10WM	BPW
2410	1074	29	37.03	3-32	0	0	83.10

Overseas tours: Ind 89/90, Aus 89/90, 91/92, 92/93, Eng 92, NZ 92/93, 93/94, WI 92/93, SA 92/93, Zim 92/93, Sharjah 88/89, 89/90, 90/91, 91/92, 92/93, 93/94, WC: Aus & NZ 91/92

Test matches: Aus 89/90 (1), WI 90/91 (2), Eng 92 (5), NZ 92/93 (1), WI 92/93 (1), Zim 93/94 (2), NZ 93/94 (1)

Best bowling against each country:			5WI	10WM
Australia	1-72	Adelaide 89/90	0	0
England	3-32	Lord's 92	0	0
New Zealand	3-79	Auckland 93/94	0	0
West Indies	2-56	Karachi 90/91	0	0
Zimbabwe	2-24	Karachi 93/94	0	0

Coopers & Lybrand world rating (bowling): 44 (283)*

DIPAK PATEL

Full name: Dipak Narshibhai Patel
Born: 25/10/58 Nairobi, Kenya
Country: New Zealand
Right-hand middle order batsman - Off break bowler
Test debut: 20/02/87 v West Indies - Basin Reserve,
Wellington

Test Career Record: *Batting & Fielding*

MAT	Inns	N/O	Runs	H/S	Avg	100s	50s	Cat
25	47	6	848	99	20.68	0	3	8

Test Career Record: *Bowling*

Balls	Runs	Wkts	Avg	Best	5WI	10WM	BPW
4050	2030	45	45.11	6-50	3	0	90.00

Overseas tours: SL 86/87, Aus 87/88, 89/90, 93/94, Pak
90/91, Zim 92/93, Sharjah 87/88, WC: Ind 87/88, RW:
Eng 92

Test matches: WI 86/87 (3), Aus 87/88 (3), Pak 88/89
(1), Aus 89/90 (1), Pak 90/91 (3), SL 90/91 (2), Eng 91/92
(3), Zim 92/93 (2), Pak 92/93 (1), Aus 92/93 (3), Aus 93/
94 (3)

Best bowling against each country:			5WI	10WM
Australia	5-93	Auckland 92/93	1	0
England	4-87	Wellington 91/92	0	0
Pakistan	2-65	Hamilton 92/93	0	0
Sri Lanka	2-90	Hamilton 90/91	0	0
West Indies	0-13	Wellington 86/87	0	0
Zimbabwe	6-50	Harare 92/93	2	0

Coopers & Lybrand world rating (bowling): 38 (336)*

PATRICK PATTERSON

Full name: Balfour Patrick Patterson
Born: 15/09/61 Happy Grove, Williamsfield, Jamaica
Country: West Indies
Right-arm fast bowler - Right-hand lower order batsman
Test debut: 21/02/86 v England - Sabina Park, Kingston, Jamaica

Test Career Record: *Batting & Fielding*

MAT	Inns	N/O	Runs	H/S	Avg	100s	50s	Cat
28	38	16	145	21*	6.59	0	0	5

Test Career Record: *Bowling*

Balls	Runs	Wkts	Avg	Best	5WI	10WM	BPW
4829	2875	93	30.91	5-24	5	0	51.92

Overseas tours: Pak 86/87, 91/92, NZ 86/87, Ind 87/88, Eng 88, 91, Aus 88/89, 91/92, 92/93, SA 92/93, Sharjah 88/89, 91/92, WC: Ind & Pak 87/88

Test matches: Eng 85/86 (5), Pak 86/87 (1), Ind 87/88 (4), Pak 87/88 (1), Eng 88 (2), Aus 88/89 (4), Eng 89/90 (1), Aus 90/91 (5), Eng 91 (3), SA 91/92 (1), Aus 92/93 (1),

Best bowling against each country:			5WI	10WM
Australia	5-39	Melbourne 88/89	2	0
England	5-81	Edgbaston 91	1	0
India	5-24	Delhi 87/88	2	0
Pakistan	2-38	Faisalabad 86/87	0	0
South Africa	1-79	Bridgetown 91/92	0	0

Coopers & Lybrand world rating (bowling): 26 (412)

MANOJ PRABHAKAR

Full name: Manoj Prabhakar
Born: 15/04/63 Ghaziabad, India
Country: India
Right-hand opening/middle order batsman - Right-arm medium bowler
Test debut: 12/12/84 v England - Feroz Shah Kotla, Delhi

Test Career Record: *Batting & Fielding*

MAT	Inns	N/O	Runs	H/S	Avg	100s	50s	Cat
33	48	7	1338	95	32.63	0	9	18

Test Career Record: *Bowling*

Balls	Runs	Wkts	Avg	Best	5WI	10WM	BPW
7121	3384	92	36.78	6-132	3	0	77.40

Overseas tours: Eng 86, 90, Pak 89/90, NZ 89/90, Aus 91/92, Zim 92/93, SA 92/93, SL 93/94, Sharjah 83/84, 86/87, 89/90, 91/92, WC: Aus & NZ 91/92, Young Ind: Zim 83/84

Test matches: Eng 84/85 (2), Pak 89/90 (4), NZ 89/90 (3), Eng 90 (3), SL 90/91 (1), Aus 91/92 (5), Zim 92/93 (1), SA 92/93 (4), Eng 92/93 (3), Zim 92/93 (1), SL 93/94 (3), SL 93/94 (3)

Best bowling against each country:			5WI	10WM
Australia	5-101	Perth 91/92	1	0
England	4-74	The Oval 90	0	0
New Zealand	3-123	Auckland 89/90	0	0
Pakistan	6-132	Faisalabad 89/90	2	0
South Africa	4-90	Johannesburg 92/93	0	0
Sri Lanka	4-82	Bangalore 93/94	0	0
Zimbabwe	3-66	Harare 92/93	0	0

Coopers & Lybrand world rating (bowling): 18 (559)

CHRIS PRINGLE

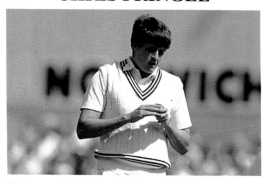

Full name: Christopher Pringle
Born: 26/01/68 Auckland, New Zealand
Country: New Zealand
Right-arm fast medium bowler - Right-hand lower order batsman
Test debut: 10/10/90 v Pakistan - National Stadium, Karachi

Test Career Record: *Batting & Fielding*								
MAT	Inns	N/O	Runs	H/S	Avg	100s	50s	Cat
8	13	2	103	24*	9.36	0	0	1

Test Career Record: *Bowling*						
Balls	Runs	Wkts	Avg	Best	5WI	10WM	BPW
1830	909	20	45.45	7-52	1	1	91.50

Overseas tours: Eng 90, Pak 90/91, Aus 90/91, SL 92/93, RW: Eng 90, 92

Test matches: Pak 90/91 (3), SL 90/91 (2), Eng 91/92 (1), SL 92/93 (1), Pak 93/94 (1)

Best bowling against each country:			5WI	10WM
England	3-127	Christchurch 91/92	0	0
Pakistan	7-52	Faisalabad 90/91	1	1
Sri Lanka	2-64	Hamilton 90/91	0	0

Coopers & Lybrand world rating (bowling): 63 (184)*

RAMIZ RAJA

Full name: Ramiz Hasan Raja
Born: 14/07/62 Lyallpur, Pakistan
Country: Pakistan
Right-hand opening batsman - Leg break bowler
Test debut: 02/03/84 v England - National Stadium, Karachi

Test Career Record: *Batting & Fielding*

MAT	Inns	N/O	Runs	H/S	Avg	100s	50s	Cat
48	78	5	2243	122	30.72	2	16	27

Overseas tours: NZ 84/5, 88/89, 92/93, Aus 84/85, 86/87, 88/89, 89/90, 91/92, 92/93, L 85/86, Ind 86/87, 89/90, Eng 87, 92, WI 87/88, 92/93, SA 9293, Zim 92/93, Ban 88/89, Sharjah 84/85, 85/86, 86/87, 88/89 89/90, 91/92, 92/93, WC: Aus & NZ 91/92, Pak under 23: SL 84/85

Test matches: Eng 83/84 (2), SL 85/86 (1), SL 85/86 (3), WI 86/87 (3), Ind 86/87 (5), Eng 87 (2), Eng 87/88 (3), WI 87/88 (3), Aus 88/89 (3), Ind 89/90 (4), Aus 89/90 (2), NZ 90/91 (3), WI 90/91 (2), SL 91/92 (3), Eng 92 (5), NZ 92/93 (1), WI 92/93 (3)

Highest score against each country:			100s	50s
Australia	64	Lahore 88/89	0	1
England	88	Old Trafford 92	0	4
India	114	Jaipur 86/87	1	4
New Zealand	78	Karachi 90/91	0	1
Sri Lanka	122	Colombo 85/86	1	4
West Indies	62	Karachi 86/87	0	2

Coopers & Lybrand world rating (batting): 54 (410)

MARK RAMPRAKASH

Full name: Mark Ravin Ramprakash
Born: 05/09/69 Bushey, Hertfordshire
Country: England
Right-hand middle order batsman - Off break bowler
Test debut: 06/06/91 v West Indies - Headingley, Leeds

Test Career Record: *Batting & Fielding*

MAT	Inns	N/O	Runs	H/S	Avg	100s	50s	Cat
10	17	1	311	64	19.43	0	1	7

Test Career Record: *Bowling*

Balls	Runs	Wkts	Avg	Best	5WI	10WM	BPW
7	8	0	-	-	-	-	-

Overseas tours: NZ 91/92, WI 93/94, Eng A: Pak & SL 90/91, WI 91/92

Test matches: WI 91 (5), SL 91 (1), Pak 92 (3), Aus 93 (1)

Highest score against each country:			100s	50s
Australia	64	The Oval 93	0	1
Pakistan	17	The Oval 92	0	0
Sri Lanka	0	Lord's 91	0	0
West Indies	29	Edgbaston 91	0	0

Coopers & Lybrand world rating (batting): 58 (365)*

ARJUNA RANATUNGA

Full name: Arjuna Ranatunga
Born: 01/12/63 Colombo, Sri Lanka
Country: Sri Lanka
Left-hand middle order batsman - Right-arm medium
bowler
Test debut: 17/02/82 v England - Saravanamuttu Stadiun,
Colombo

Test Career Record: *Batting & Fielding*

MAT	Inns	N/O	Runs	H/S	Avg	100s	50s	Cat
49	82	4	2720	135*	34.87	4	17	22

Test Career Record: *Bowling*

Balls	Runs	Wkts	Avg	Best	5WI	10WM	BPW
2096	911	14	65.07	2-17	0	0	149.71

Overseas tours: Pak 81/82, 85/86, 91/92, Zim 82/83, Ind
82/83, 86/87, 89/90, 90/91, 93/94, Eng 84, 88, Aus 84/85,
87/88, 89/90, NZ 90/91, Ban 88/89, Sharjah 83/84, 85/86,
86/87, 87/88, 88/89, 89/90, 90/91, 92/93, 93/94, WC: Eng
83, Ind & Pak 87/88, Aus & NZ 91/92, SL under 23: Pak
83/84

Test matches: Eng 81/82 (1), Pak 81/82 (2), Ind 82/83
(1), Aus 82/83 (1), NZ 83/84 (3), Eng 84 (1), Ind 85/86
(3), Pak 85/86 (3), Pak 85/86 (3), Ind 86/87 (1), NZ 86/87
(1), Aus 87/88 (1), Eng 88 (1), Aus 89/90 (2), Ind 90/91
(1), NZ 90/91 (3), Pak 91/92 (3), Aus 92/93 (3), NZ 92/93
(2), Eng 92/93 (1), Ind 93/94 (3), SA 93/94 (3), WI 93/94
(1), Ind 93/94 (3)

Highest score against each country:			100s	50s
Australia	127	Colombo 92/93	1	2
England	84	Lord's 84	0	4
India	111	Colombo 85/86	1	3
New Zealand	76	Colombo 92/93	0	4
Pakistan	135*	Colombo 85/86	1	3
South Africa	131	Moratuwa 93/94	1	1
West Indies	31	Moratuwa 93/94	0	0

Coopers & Lybrand world rating (batting): 38 (511)

RASHID LATIF

Full name: Rashid Latif
Born: 14/10/08 Karachi, Pakistan
Country: Pakistan
Right-hand middle order batsman - Wicket-Keeper - Leg break bowler
Test debut: 06/08/92 v England - The Oval, London

Test Career Record: *Batting & Fielding*									
MAT	*Inns*	*N/O*	*Runs*	*H/S*	*Avg*	*100s*	*50s*	*Cat*	*St*
9	12	3	361	68*	40.11	0	3	26	3

Overseas tours: Eng 92, Aus 92/93, NZ 92/93, 93/94, WI 92/93, Sharjah 93/94

Test matches: Eng 92 (1), NZ 92/93 (1), WI 92/93 (1), Zim 93/94 (3) N/Z 93/94 (3)

Highest score against each country:			100s	50s
England	50	The Oval 92	0	1
New Zealand	33	Hamilton 92/93	0	0
West Indies	4	St John's 92/93	0	0
Zimbabwe	68*	Karachi 93/94	0	2

Coopers & Lybrand world rating (batting): 51 (419)*

PAUL REIFFEL

Full name: Paul Ronald Reiffel
Born: 19/04/66 Box Hill, Melbourne, Victoria, Australia
Country: Australia
Right-arm fast medium bowler - Right-hand lower order batsman
Test debut: 01/02/92 v India - W.A.C.A. Ground, Perth

Test Career Record: Batting & Fielding								
MAT	Inns	N/O	Runs	H/S	Avg	100s	50s	Cat
11	12	3	214	51	23.77	0	1	4

Test Career Record: Bowling							
Balls	Runs	Wkts	Avg	Best	5WI	10WM	BPW
2200	973	29	33.55	6-71	2	0	75.86

Overseas tours: NZ 92/93, Eng 93, Aus B: Zim 91/92

Test matches: Ind 91/92 (1), NZ 92/93 (3), Eng 93 (3), NZ 93/94 (2), SA 93/94 (2)

Best bowling against each country:			5WI	10WM
England	6-71	Edgbaston 93	2	0
India	2-34	Perth 91/92	0	0
New Zealand	2-27	Christchurch 92/93	0	0
South Africa	1-36	Adelaide 93/94	0	0

Coopers & Lybrand worldd rating (bowler): 22 (468)*

'JONTY' RHODES

Full name: Jonathan Neil Rhodes
Born: 26/07/69 Pietermaritzburg, South Africa
Country: South Africa
Right-hand middle order batsman
Test debut: 18/04/92 v West Indies - Kensington Oval, Bridgetown

Test Career Record: *Batting & Fielding*								
MAT	Inns	N/O	Runs	H/S	Avg	100s	50s	Cat
10	17	4	544	101*	41.84	1	3	6
Test Career Record: *Bowling*								
Balls	Runs	Wkts	Avg		Best	5WI	10WM	BPW
6	5	0	-		-	-	-	-

Overseas tours: WI 91/92, SL 93/94, Ind 93/94, Aus 93/94, WC: Aus & NZ 91/92

Test matches: Ind 92/93 (4), SL 93/94 (3), Aus 93/94 (3)

Highest score against each opposition:			100s	50s
Australia	76*	Sydney 93/94	0	1
India	91	Johannesburg 92/93	0	2
Sri Lanka	101*	Moratuwa 93/94	1	0

Coopers & Lybrand world rating (batting): 34 (548)*

DAVID RICHARDSON

Full name: David John Richardson
Born: 16/09/59 Johannesburg, South Africa
Country: South Africa
Right-hand middle order batsman - Wicket-Keeper
Test debut: 18/04/92 v West Indies - Kensington Oval,
Bridgetown

Test Career Record: *Batting & Fielding*									
MAT	*Inns*	*N/O*	*Runs*	*H/S*	*Avg*	*100s*	*50s*	*Cat*	*St*
11	16	1	239	62	15.93	0	2	48	0

Overseas tours: Ind 91/92, 93/94, WI 91/92, SL 93/94,
Aus 93/94, WC: Aus & NZ 91/92

Test matches: WI 91/92 (1), Ind 92/93 (4), SL 93/94 (3),
Aus 93/94 (3)

Highest score against each country:			100s	50s
Australia	24	Sydney 93/94	0	0
India	50	Johannesburg 92/93	0	1
Sri Lanka	62	Colombo 93/94	0	1
West Indies	8	Bridgetown 91/92	0	0

Coopers & Lybrand world rating (batting): 85 (225)*

RITCHIE RICHARDSON

Full name: Richard Benjamin Richardson
Born: 12/01/62 Five Islands Village, Antigua
Country: West India
Right-hand middle order batsman - Right-arm medium bowler
Test debut: 24/11/83 v India - Wankhede Stadium, Bombay

Test Career Record: *Batting & Fielding*

MAT	Inns	N/O	Runs	H/S	Avg	100s	50s	Cat
72	123	10	5282	194	46.74	15	24	78

Test Career Record: *Bowling*

Balls	Runs	Wkts	Avg	Best	5WI	10WM	BPW
66	18	0	-	-	-	-	-

Overseas tours: Ind 83/84, 87/88, 89/90, 93/94, Aus 83/84, 84/85, 86/87, 88/89, 91/92, 92/93, Eng 84, 88, 91, Pak 85/86, 86/87, 90/91, 91/92, NZ 86/87, SA 92/93, SL 93/94, Sharjah 85/86, 86/87, 88/89, 89/90, 91/92, 93/94, WC: Ind & Pak 87/88, Aus & NZ 91/92, RW: Eng 90, 92

Test matches: Ind 83/84 (1), Aus 83/84 (5), Aus 84/85 (5), NZ 84/85 (4), Eng 85/86 (5), Pak 86/87 (3), NZ 86/87 (3), Ind 87/88 (4), Pak 87/88 (3), Eng 88 (3), Aus 88/89 (5), Ind 88/89 (4), Eng 89/90 (4), Pak 90/91 (3), Aus 90/91 (5), Eng 91 (5), SA 91/92 (1), Aus 92/93 (5), Pak 92/93 (3), SL 93/94 (1)

Highest score against each country:			100s	50s
Australia	182	Georgetown 90/91	8	7
England	160	Bridgetown 85/86	4	3
India	194	Georgetown 88/89	2	5
New Zealand	185	Georgetown 84/85	1	2
Pakistan	75	Georgetown 87/88	0	6
South Africa	44	Bridgetown 91/92	0	0
Sri Lanka	51	Moratuwa 93/94	0	1

Coopers & Lybrand world rating (batting): 3 (785)

'JACK' RUSSELL

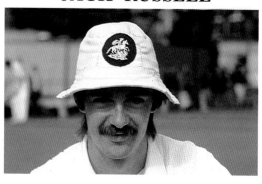

Full name: Robert Charles Russell
Born: 15/08/63 Stroud, Gloucestershire
Country: England
Left-hand middle order batsman - Wicket-Keeper
Test debut: 25/08/88 v Sri Lanka - Lord's, London

Test Career Record: *Batting & Fielding*								
MAT	Inns	N/O	Runs	H/S	Avg	100s	50s	Cat St
31	49	10	1060	128*	27.17	1	3	80 8

Overseas tours: Pak 87/88, Ind 89/90, WI 89/90, 93/94,
Aus 90/91, NZ 90/91, 91/92, Eng A: Aus 92/93

Test matches: SL 88 (1), Aus 89 (6), WI 89/90 (4), NZ
90 (3), Ind 90 (3), Aus 90/91 (3), WI 91 (4), SL 91 (1),
NZ 91/92 (3), Pak 92 (3)

Highest score against each country:			100s	50s
Australia	128*	Old Trafford 89	1	1
India	35	The Oval 90	0	0
New Zealand	43	Edgbaston 90	0	0
Pakistan	29*	Edgbaston 92	0	0
Sri Lanka	94	Lord's 88	0	1
West Indies	55	Bridgetown 89/90	0	1

KEN RUTHERFORD

Full name: Kenneth Robert Rutherford
Born: 26/10/65 Dunedin, New Zealand
Country: New Zealand
Right-hand middle order batsman - Right-arm medium
bowler
Test debut: 29/03/85 v West Indies - Queens Park Oval,
Port of Spain

Test Career Record: *Batting & Fielding*

MAT	Inns	N/O	Runs	H/S	Avg	100s	50s	Cat
44	77	7	1901	107*	27.15	3	13	29

Test Career Record: *Bowling*

Balls	Runs	Wkts	Avg	Best	5WI	10WM	BPW
256	161	1	161.00	1-38	0	0	256.00

Overseas tours: WI 84/85, SL 85/86, 86/87, 92/93, Eng
86, 90, Aus 87/88, 90/91, 93/94, Ind 88/89, Pak 90/91,
Zim 92/93, Sharjah 85/86, 87/88, 89/90, WC: Ind 87/88,
Young NZ: Zim 84/85, 88/89

Test matches: WI 84/85 (4), Aus 85/86 (3), Eng 86 (1),
WI 86/87 (2), SL 86/87 (1), Aus 87/88 (1), Eng 87/88 (2),
Ind 88/89 (2), Ind 89/90 (3), Aus 89/90 (1), Eng 90 (2),
Pak 90/91 (3), SL 90/91 (3), Eng 91/92 (2), Zim 92/93
(2), SL 92/93 (2), Pak 92/93 (1), Aus 92/93 (3), Aus 93/
94 (3), Pak 93/94 (3)

Highest score against each country:			100s	50s
Australia	102	Christchurch 92/93	1	6
England	107*	Wellington 87/88	1	0
India	69	Christchurch 89/90	0	1
Pakistan	79	Karachi 90/91	0	3
Sri Lanka	105	Moratuwa 92/93	1	1
West Indies	12	Auckland 86/87	0	0
Zimbabwe	89	Harare 92/93	0	2

Coopers & Lybrand world rating (batting): 24= (583)

SALIM MALIK

Full name: Salim Malik
Born: 16/04/63 Lahore, Pakistan
Country: Pakistan
Right-hand middle order batsman - Right arm medium or
leg break bowler
Test debut: 05/03/82 v Sri Lanka - National Stadium,
Karachi

Test Career Record: *Batting & Fielding*

MAT	Inns	N/O	Runs	H/S	Avg	100s	50s	Cat
75	108	18	3967	165	44.07	11	21	52

Test Career Record: *Bowling*

Balls	Runs	Wkts	Avg	Best	5WI	10WM	BPW
308	144	5	28.80	1-3	0	0	61.60

Overseas tours: Aus 81/82, 83/84, 84/85, 88/89, 89/90,
91/92, 92/93, Eng 82, 87, 92, Ind 83/84, 86/87, 89/90, NZ
84/85, 88/89, 92/93, 93/94, SL 85/86, WI 87/88, SA 92/
93, Ban 88/89, Sharjah 83/84, 84/85, 85/86, 86/87, 88/89,
89/90, 90/91, 91/92, WC: Aus & NZ 91/92, Pak under 23:
SL 84/85

Test matches: SL 81/82 (2), Ind 82/83 (6), Ind 83/84 (2),
Aus 83/84 (3), Eng 83/84 (3), Ind 84/85 (2), NZ 84/85 (3),
NZ 84/85 (3), SL 85/86 (3), SL 85/86 (3), WI 86/87 (1),
Ind 86/87 (5), Eng 87 (5), Eng 87/88 (3), WI 87/88 (3),
Aus 88/89 (3), NZ 88/89 (2), Ind 89/90 (4), Aus 89/90
(1), NZ 90/91 (3), WI 90/91 (3), SL 91/92 (3), Eng 92 (5),
NZ 92/93 (1), NZ 93/94 (3)

Highest score against each country:			100s	50s
Australia	77	Adelaide 83/84	0	3
England	165	Edgbaston 92	3	8
India	107	Faisalabad 82/83	3	2
New Zealand	140	Wellington 93/94	2	4
Sri Lanka	101	Sialkot 91/92	2	1
West Indies	102	Karachi 90/91	1	3

Coopers & Lybrand world rating (batting): 7 (685)

IAN SALISBURY

Full name: Ian David Kenneth Salisbury
Born: 21/01/70 Northampton, England
Country: England
Leg break and googly bowler - Right-hand lower order
batsman
Test debut: 18/06/92 v Pakistan - Lord's, London

Test Career Record: *Batting & Fielding*								
MAT	*Inns*	*N/O*	*Runs*	*H/S*	*Avg*	*100s*	*50s*	*Cat*
4	7	0	136	50	19.42	0	1	2

Test Career Record: *Bowling*							
Balls	*Runs*	*Wkts*	*Avg*	*Best*	*5WI*	*10WM*	*BPW*
733	536	8	67.00	3-49	0	0	91.62

Overseas tours: Ind 92/93, SL 92/93, WI 93/94, Eng A:
Pak & SL 90/91, WI 91/92

Test matches: Pak 92 (2), Ind 92/93 (2)

Best bowling against each country:		5WI	10WM
India	2-142 Madras 92/93	0	0
Pakistan	3-49 Lord's 92	0	0

Coopers & Lybrand world rating (bowling): 80 (51)*

BRETT SCHULTZ

Full name: Brett Nolan Schultz
Born: 26/08/70 East London, South Africa
Country: South Africa
Left-arm fast bowler - Left-hand lower order batsman
Test debut: 13/11/92 v India - Kingsmead, Durban, South Africa

Test Career Record: *Batting & Fielding*

MAT	Inns	N/O	Runs	H/S	Avg	100s	50s	Cat
5	5	2	6	6	2.00	0	0	0

Test Career Record: *Bowling*

Balls	Runs	Wkts	Avg	Best	5WI	10WM	BPW
1055	427	24	17.79	5-48	2	0	43.95

Overseas tours: SL 93/94

Test matches: Ind 92/93 (2), SL 93/94 (3)

Best bowling against each country:			5WI	10WM
India	2-37	Port Elizabeth 92/93	0	0
Sri Lanka	5-48	Colombo 93/94	2	0

Coopers & Lybrand world rating (bowling): 15 (600)*

SHOAIB MOHAMMAD

Full name: Shoaib Mohammad
Born: 08/01/62 Karachi, Pakistan
Country: Pakistan
Right-hand opening/middle order batsman - Off break bowler
Test debut: 24/09/83 v India - Burlton Park, Jullundur

Test Career Record: *Batting & Fielding*

MAT	Inns	N/O	Runs	H/S	Avg	100s	50s	Cat
42	63	7	2622	203*	46.82	7	12	21

Test Career Record: *Bowling*

Balls	Runs	Wkts	Avg	Best	5WI	10WM	BPW
282	130	5	26.00	2-8	0	0	56.40

Overseas tours: Ind 83/84, 86/87, 89/90, NZ 84/85, 88/89, SL 85/86, Aus 86/87, 88/89, 89/90, Eng 87, 92, WI 87/88, Ban 88/89, SA 92/93, Zim 92/93, Sharjah 84/85, 86/87, 88/89, 89/90
Test matches: Ind 83/84 (2), Eng 83/84 (1), Pak 84/85 (1), NZ 84/85 (1), SL 85/86 (1), Ind 86/87 (3), Eng 87 (4), Eng 87/88 (1), WI 87/88 (3), Aus 88/89 (3), NZ 88/89 (2), Ind 89/90 (4), Aus 89/90 (3), NZ 90/91 (3), WI 90/91 (3), SL 91/92 (3), Eng 92 (1), Zim 93/94 (3)

Highest score against each country:			100s	50s
Australia	94	Karachi 88/89	0	2
England	80	Lahore 83/84	0	3
India	203*	Lahore 89/90	2	2
New Zealand	203*	Karachi 90/91	5	0
Sri Lanka	43	Sialkot 91/92	0	0
West Indies	86	Karachi 90/91	0	3
Zimbabwe	81	Karachi 93/94	0	2

Coopers & Lybrand world rating (batting): 14 (640)

NAVJOT SIDHU

Full name: Navjot Singh Sidhu
Born: 20/10/63 Patiala, India
Country: India
Right-hand opening batsman
Test debut: 12/11/83 v West Indies - Gujarat Stadium,
Ahmedabad

Test Career Record: *Batting & Fielding*								
MAT	Inns	N/O	Runs	H/S	Avg	100s	50s	Cat
30	44	2	1681	124	40.02	5	8	7

Test Career Record: *Bowling*							
Balls	Runs	Wkts	Avg	Best	5WI	10WM	BPW
6	9	0	-	-	-	-	-

Overseas tours: WI 88/89, Pak 89/90, NZ 89/90, Eng 90,
Aus 91/92, SL 93/94, Ban 88/89, Sharjah 87/88, 88/89,
89/90, 91/92

Test matches: WI 83/84 (2), NZ 88/89 (3), WI 88/89 (4),
Pak 89/90 (4), NZ 89/90 (1), Eng 90 (3), Aus 91/92 (3),
Eng 92/93 (3), Zim 92/93 (1), SL 93/94 (3), SL 93/94 (3)

Highest score against each country:			100s	50s
Australia	35	Adelaide 91/92	0	0
	35	Perth 91/92		
England	106	Madras 92/93	1	1
New Zealand	116	Bangalore 88/89	1	1
Pakistan	97	Sialkot 89/90	0	3
Sri Lanka	124	Lucknow 93/94	2	2
West Indies	116	Kingston 88/89	1	0
Zimbabwe	61	Delhi 92/93	0	1

Coopers & Lybrand world rating (batting): 11 (647)

PHIL SIMMONS

Full name: Philip Verant Simmons
Born: 18/04/63 Arima, Trinidad
Country: West Indies
Right-hand opening batsman - Right-arm medium bowler
Test debut: 11/01/88 v India - Chidambaram Stadium, Chepauk, Madras

Test Career Record: *Batting & Fielding*

MAT	Inns	N/O	Runs	H/S	Avg	100s	50s	Cat
17	31	1	757	110	25.23	1	2	15

Test Career Record: *Bowling*

Balls	Runs	Wkts	Avg	Best	5WI	10WM	BPW
378	154	2	77.00	2-34	0	0	189.00

Overseas tours: Ind 87/88, 89/90, 93/94, Eng 88, 91, Aus 92/93, SA 92/93, SL 93/94, Sharjah 89/90, 91/92, 93/94, WC: Pak & Ind 87/88, Aus & NZ 91/92, RW: Eng 92, Young WI: Zim 86/87

Test matches: Ind 87/88 (1), Pak 87/88 (1), Eng 91 (5), SA 91/92 (1), Aus 92/93 (5), Pak 92/93 (3), SL 93/94 (1)

Highest score against each country:			100s	50s
Australia	110	Melbourne 92/93	1	1
England	38	Headingley 91	0	0
India	14	Madras 87/88	0	0
Pakistan	87	Bridgetown 92/93	0	1
South Africa	35	Bridgetown 91/92	0	0
Sri Lanka	17	Moratuwa 93/94	0	0

Coopers & Lybrand world rating (batting): 32= (549)

MICHAEL SLATER

Full name: Michael Jonathon Slater
Born: 21/02/70 Wagga Wagga, New South Wales, Australia
Country: Australia
Right-hand opening batsman
Test debut: 03/06/93 v England - Old Trafford, Manchester

Test Career Record: *Batting & Fielding*								
MAT	*Inns*	*N/O*	*Runs*	*H/S*	*Avg*	*100s*	*50s*	*Cat*
12	19	0	906	168	47.68	2	5	2

Overseas tours: Eng 93

Test matches: Eng 93 (6), NZ 93/94 (3), SA 93/94 (3)

Highest score against each country:			100s	50s
England	152	Lord's 93	1	2
New Zealand	168	Hobart 93/94	1	1
South Africa	92	Sydney 93/94	0	2

Coopers & Lybrand world rating (batting): 20= (598)*

ROBIN SMITH

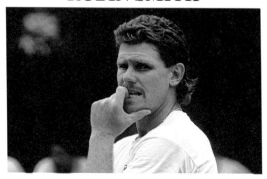

Full name: Robin Arnold Smith
Born: 13/09/63 Durban, South Africa
Country: England
Right-hand middle order batsman - Off break bowler
Test debut: 21/07/88 v West Indies - Headingley, Leeds

Test Career Record: *Batting & Fielding*								
MAT	Inns	N/O	Runs	H/S	Avg	100s	50s	Cat
45	84	14	3237	148*	46.24	8	22	31

Test Career Record: *Bowling*							
Balls	Runs	Wkts	Avg	Best	5WI	10WM	BPW
24	6	0	-	-	-	-	-

Overseas tours: Ind 89/90, 92/93, WI 89/90, 93/94, Aus 90/91, NZ 90/91, 91/92, SL 92/93, WC: Aus & NZ 91/92

Test matches: WI 88 (2), SL 88 (1), Aus 89 (5), WI 89/90 (4), NZ 90 (3), Ind 90 (3), Aus 90/91 (5), WI 91 (4), SL 91 (1) NZ 91/92 (3), Pak 92 (5), Ind 92/93 (3), SL 92/93 (1), Aus 93 (5)

Highest score against each country:			100s	50s
Australia	143	Old Trafford 89	2	7
India	121*	Old Trafford 90	2	4
New Zealand	96	Christchurch 91/92	0	4
Pakistan	127	Edgbaston 92	1	1
Sri Lanka	128	Colombo 92/93	1	1
West Indies	148*	Lord's 91	2	5

Coopers & Lybrand world rating (batting): 16 (611)

ALEC STEWART

Full name: Alec James Stewart
Born: 08/04/63 Merton, Surrey
Country: England
Right-hand opening/middle order batsman - Wicket-
Keeper
Test debut: 24/02/89 v West Indies - Sabina Park,
Kingston

Test Career Record: *Batting & Fielding*									
MAT	*Inns*	*N/O*	*Runs*	*H/S*	*Avg*	*100s*	*50s*	*Cat*	*St*
32	60	4	2083	190	37.19	4		11	46	4

Overseas tours: Ind 89/90, 92/93, WI 89/90, 93/94, Aus
90/91, NZ 90/91, 91/92, SL 92/93, WC: Aus & NZ 91/92

Test matches: WI 89/90 (4), NZ 90 (3), Aus 90/91 (5),
WI 91 (1), SL 91 (1), NZ 91/92 (3), Pak 92 (5), Ind 92/93
(3), SL 92/93 (1), Aus 93 (6)

Highest score against each country:			100s	50s
Australia	91	Sydney 90/91	0	5
India	74	Madras 92/93	0	1
New Zealand	148	Christchurch 91/92	2	2
Pakistan	190	Edgbaston 92	1	2
Sri Lanka	113*	Lord's 91	1	1
West Indies	45	Bridgetown 89/90	0	0

Coopers & Lybrand world rating (batting): 27 (567)

MURPHY SU'A

Full name: Murphy Logo Su'a
Born: 07/11/66 Wanganui, New Zealand
Country: New Zealand
Left-arm fast medium bowler - Left-hand lower order batsman
Test debut: 30/01/91 v England - Eden Park, Auckland

Test Career Record: *Batting & Fielding*

MAT	Inns	N/O	Runs	H/S	Avg	100s	50s	Cat
11	15	4	131	44	11.90	0	0	6

Test Career Record: *Bowling*

Balls	Runs	Wkts	Avg	Best	5WI	10WM	BPW
2298	1058	32	33.06	5-73	2	0	71.81

Overseas tours: Zim 92/93, SL 92/93, Aus 93/94

Test matches: Eng 91/92 (2), Zim 92/93 (2), SL 92/93 (2), Pak 92/93 (1), Aus 92/93 (2), Aus 93/94 (2)

Best bowling against each country:			5WI	10WM
Australia	2-72	Perth 93/94	0	0
England	3-87	Wellington 91/92	0	0
Pakistan	5-73	Hamilton 92/93	1	0
Sri Lanka	2-50	Colombo 92/93	0	0
Zimbabwe	5-85	Harare 92/93	1	0

Coopers & Lybrand world rating (bowling): 42 (313)*

MARK TAYLOR

Full name: Mark Anthony Taylor
Born. 27/10/64 Leeton, New South Wales, Australia
Country: Australia
Left-hand opening batsman - Right arm medium bowler
Test debut: 26/01/89 v West Indies - Sydney Cricket
Ground

Test Career Record: *Batting & Fielding*

MAT	Inns	N/O	Runs	H/S	Avg	100s	50s	Cat
52	93	6	4178	219	48.02	12	23	71

Test Career Record: *Bowling*

Balls	Runs	Wkts	Avg	Best	5WI	10WM	BPW
24	15	0	-	-	-	-	-

Overseas tours: Eng 89, 93, NZ 89/90, 92/93, WI 90/91,
SL 92/93, Sharjah 89/90, Aus B: Zim 91/92

Test matches: WI 88/89 (2), Eng 89 (6), NZ 89/90 (1),
SL 89/90 (2), Pak 89/90 (3), NZ 89/90 (1), Eng 90/91 (5),
WI 90/91 (5), Ind 91/92 (5), SL 92/93 (3), WI 92/93 (4),
NZ 92/93 (3), Eng 93 (6), NZ 93/94 (3), SA 93/94 (3)

Highest score against each country:			100s	50s
England	219	Trent Bridge 89	4	8
India	100	Adelaide 91/92	1	3
New Zealand	142*	Perth 93/94	1	4
Pakistan	101*	Sydney 89/90	2	3
South Africa	170	Melbourne 93/94	1	1
Sri Lanka	164	Brisbane 89/90	2	0
West Indies	144	St John's 90/91	1	4

Coopers & Lybrand world rating (batting): 12 (652)

SACHIN TENDULKAR

Full name: Sachin Ramesh Tendulkar
Born: 24/04/73 Bombay, India
Country: India
Right-hand middle order batsman - Right-arm medium
bowler
Test debut: 15/11/89 v Pakistan - National Stadium,
Karachi

Test Career Record: *Batting & Fielding*								
MAT	Inns	N/O	Runs	H/S	Avg	100s	50s	Cat
31	43	4	1969	165	50.48	7	10	23
Test Career Record: *Bowling*							
Balls	Runs	Wkts	Avg	Best	5WI	10WM	BPW
408	172	4	43.00	2-10	0	0	102.00

Overseas tours: Pak 89/90, NZ 89/90, Eng 90, Aus 91/
92, Zim 92/93, SA 92/93, SL 93/94, Sharjah 89/90, 91/92,
WC: Aus & NZ 91/92, RW: Eng 91

Test matches: Pak 89/90 (4), NZ 89/90 (3), Eng 90 (3),
SL 90/91 (1), Aus 91/92 (5), Zim 92/93 (1), SA 92/93 (4),
Eng 92/93 (3), Zim 92/93 (1), SL 93/94 (3), SL 93/94 (3)

Highest score against each opposition:			100s	50s
Australia	148*	Sydney 91/92	2	0
England	165	Madras 92/93	2	3
New Zealand	88	Napier 89/90	0	1
Pakistan	59	Faisalabad 89/90	0	2
South Africa	111	Johannesburg 92/93	1	1
Sri Lanka	142	Lucknow 93/94	2	2
Zimbabwe	62	Delhi 92/93	0	1

Coopers & Lybrand world rating (batting): 4 (765)

GRAHAM THORPE

Full name: Graham Paul Thorpe
Born: 01/08/69 Farnham, Surrey
Country: England
Left-hand middle order batsman - Right-arm medium bowler
Test debut: 01/07/93 v Australia - Trent Bridge, Nottingham

Test Career Record: *Batting & Fielding*

MAT	Inns	N/O	Runs	H/S	Avg	100s	50s	Cat
3	6	1	230	114*	46.00	1	1	5

Test Career Record: *Bowling*

Balls	Runs	Wkts	Avg	Best	5WI	10WM	BPW
36	14	0	-	-	-	-	-

Overseas tours: WI 93/94, Eng A: Zim 89/90, Pak & SL 90/91, WI 91/92, Aus 92/93

Test matches: Aus 93 (3)

Highest score against each country:		100s	50s
Australia	112* Trent Bridge 93	1	1

Coopers & Lybrand world rating (batting): 62 (351)*

HASHAN TILLEKERATNE

Full name: Hashan Prasantha Tillekeratne
Born: 14/07/67 Colombo, Sri Lanka
Country: Sri Lanka
Left-hand middle order batsman - Wicket-Keeper - Off
break bowler
Test debut: 16/12/89 v Australia - Bellerive Oval, Hobart

Test Career Record: *Batting & Fielding*

MAT	Inns	N/O	Runs	H/S	Avg	100s	50s	Cat
23	37	5	1146	93*	35.81	0	8	52

Test Career Record: *Bowling*

Balls	Runs	Wkts	Avg	Best	5WI	10WM	BPW
18	6	0	-	-	-	-	-

Overseas tours: Aus 87/88, 89/90, Eng 88, 90, 91, Ind
89/90, 90/91, 93/94, NZ 90/91, Pak 91/92, Ban 88/89,
Sharjah 86/87, 88/89, 89/90, 90/91, 92/93, 93/94, WC:
Aus & NZ 91/92, SL B: Zim 87/88
Test matches: Aus 89/90 (1), Ind 90/91 (1), NZ 90/91
(3), Eng 91 (1), Pak 91/92 (3), Aus 92/93 (1), NZ 92/93
(2), Eng 92/93 (1), Ind 93/94 (3), SA 93/94 (3), WI 93/94
(1), Ind 93/94 (3)

Highest score against each country:			100s	50s
Australia	82	Moratuwa 92/93	0	1
England	93*	Colombo 92/93	0	1
India	86	Colombo 93/94	0	4
	93	Colombo 92/93	0	1
	9	Sialkot 91/92	0	0
	2	Moratuwa 93/94	0	1
	9*	Moratuwa 93/94	0	0

and world rating (batting): 28 (565)

PHIL TUFNELL

Full name: Philip Clive Roderick Tufnell
Born: 29/04/66 Barnet, Hertfordshire
Country: England
Left-arm slow bowler - Right-hand lower order batsman
Test debut: 26/12/90 v Australia - Melbourne Cricket Ground

Test Career Record: *Batting & Fielding*

MAT	Inns	N/O	Runs	H/S	Avg	100s	50s	Cat
15	23	13	56	22*	5.60	0	0	5

Test Career Record: *Bowling*

Balls	Runs	Wkts	Avg	Best	5WI	10WM	BPW
4124	1826	50	36.52	7-47	4	1	82.48

Overseas tours: Aus 90/91, NZ 90/91, 91/92, Ind 92/93, SL 92/93, WI 93/94, WC: Aus & NZ 91/92

Test matches: Aus 90/91 (4), WI 91 (1), SL 91 (1), NZ 91/92 (3), Pak 92 (1), Ind 92/93 (2), SL 92/93 (1), Aus 93 (2)

Best bowling against each country:			5WI	10WM
Australia	5-61	Sydney 90/91	1	0
India	4-142	Bombay 92/93	0	0
New Zealand	7-47	Christchurch 91/92	1	1
Pakistan	1-87	The Oval 92	0	0
Sri Lanka	5-94	Lord's 91	1	0
West Indies	6-25	The Oval 91	1	0

Coopers & Lybrand world rating (bowling): 23 (449)

VENKATAPATHY RAJU

Full name: Sagi Lakshmi Venkatapathy Raju
Born: 09/07/69 Hyderabad, India
Country: India
Left-arm slow bowler - Right-hand lower order batsman
Test debut: 02/02/90 v New Zealand - Lancaster Park, Christchurch

Test Career Record: *Batting & Fielding*

MAT	Inns	N/O	Runs	H/S	Avg	100s	50s	Cat
17	21	8	186	31	14.30	0	0	5

Test Career Record: *Bowling*

Balls	Runs	Wkts	Avg	Best	5WI	10WM	BPW
4901	1743	58	30.05	6-12	3	1	84.50

Overseas tours: NZ 89/90, Eng 90, Aus 91/92, Zim 92/93, SA 92/93, SL 93/94, Sharjah 91/92, WC: Aus & NZ 91/92

Test matches: NZ 89/90 (2), SL 90/91 (1), Aus 91/92 (4), Zim 92/93 (1), SA 92/93 (2), Eng 92/93 (3), SL 93/94 (1), SL 93/94 (3)

Best bowling against each country:			5WI	10WM
Australia	3-11	Adelaide 91/92	0	0
England	4-103	Madras 92/93	0	0
New Zealand	3-86	Christchurch 89/90	0	0
South Africa	3-73	Port Elizabeth 92/93	0	0
Sri Lanka	6-12	Chandigarh 90/91	3	1
Zimbabwe	0-17	Harare 92/93	0	0

Coopers & Lybrand world rating (bowling): 17 (574)

COURTNEY WALSH

Full name: Courtney Andrew Walsh
Born: 30/10/62 Kingston, Jamaica
Country: West Indies
Right-arm fast bowler - Right-hand lower order batsman
Test debut: 09/11/84 v Australia - WACA Ground, Perth

Test Career Record: *Batting & Fielding*

MAT	Inns	N/O	Runs	H/S	Avg	100s	50s	Cat
60	82	25	518	30*	9.08	0	0	8

Test Career Record: *Bowling*

Balls	Runs	Wkts	Avg	Best	5WI	10WM	BPW
11826	5178	203	25.50	6-62	5	1	58.25

Overseas tours: Eng 84, 88, 91, Aus 84/85, 86/87, 88/89, 92/93, Pak 85/86, 86/87, 90/91, NZ 86/87, Ind 87/88, 89/90, 93/94, SA 92/93, SL 93/94, Sharjah 85/86, 86/87, 88/89, 89/90, 91/92, 93/94, WC: Ind & Pak 87/88, RW: Eng 87, Young WI: Zim 83/84

Test matches: Aus 84/85 (5), NZ 84/85 (1), Eng 85/86 (1), Pak 86/87 (3), NZ 86/87 (3), Ind 87/88 (4), Pak 87/88 (3), Eng 88 (5), Aus 88/89 (5), Ind 88/89 (4), Eng 89/90 (3), Pak 90/91 (3), Aus 90/91 (5), Eng 91 (5), SA 91/92 (1), Aus 92/93 (5), Pak 92/93 (3), SL 93/94 (1),

Best bowling against each country:			5WI	10WM
Australia	4-14	Bridgetown 90/91	0	0
England	5-68	Kingston 89/90	1	0
India	6-62	Kingston 88/89	3	1
New Zealand	5-73	Auckland 86/87	1	0
Pakistan	4-21	Lahore 86/87	0	0
South Africa	4-31	Bridgetown 91/92	0	0
Sri Lanka	1-40	Moratuwa 92/93	0	0

Coopers & Lybrand world rating (bowling): 16 (595)

WAQAR YOUNIS

Full name: Waqar Younis
Born: 16/11/71 Vehari, Pakistan
Country: Pakistan
Right-arm fast bowler - Right-hand lower order batsman
Test debut: 15/11/89 v India - National Stadium, Karachi

Test Career Record: *Batting & Fielding*

MAT	Inns	N/O	Runs	H/S	Avg	100s	50s	Cat
29	35	6	254	29	8.75	0	0	3

Test Career Record: *Bowling*

Balls	Runs	Wkts	Avg	Best	5WI	10WM	BPW
6082	3152	166	18.98	7-76	17	3	36.63

Overseas tours: Aus 89/90, 92/93, Ind 89/90, WI 91/92, 92/93, Eng 92, NZ 92/93, 93/94, SA 92/93, Zim 92/93, Sharjah 89/90, 90/91, 91/92, 92/93, 93/94

Test matches: Ind 89/90 (2), Aus 89/90 (3), NZ 90/91 (3), WI 90/91 (3), SL 91/92 (3), Eng 92 (5), NZ 92/93 (1), WI 92/93 (3), Zim 93/94 (3), NZ 93/94 (3)

Best bowling against each country:			5WI	10WM
Australia	2-66	Adelaide 89/90	0	0
England	5-52	The Oval 92	3	0
India	4-80	Karachi 89/90	0	0
New Zealand	7-76	Faisalabad 90/91	5	2
Sri Lanka	5-65	Faisalabad 91/92	2	0
West Indies	5-46	Faisalabad 90/91	3	0
Zimbabwe	7-91	Karachi 93/94	4	1

Coopers & Lybrand world rating (bowling): 1 (909)

SHANE WARNE

Full name: Shane Keith Warne
Born: 13/09/69 - Ferntree Gully, Melbourne
Country: Australia
Leg break and googly bowler - Right-hand lower order batsman
Test debut: 02/01/92 v India - Sydney Cricket Ground

Test Career Record: *Batting & Fielding*

MAT	Inns	N/O	Runs	H/S	Avg	100s	50s	Cat
23	29	7	399	74*	18.13	0	1	16

Test Career Record: *Bowling*

Balls	Runs	Wkts	Avg	Best	5WI	10WM	BPW
6840	2444	101	24.19	7-52	5	1	67.72

Overseas tours: SL 92/93, NZ 92/93, Eng 93, Aus B: Zim 91/92

Test matches: Ind 91/92 (2), SL 92/93 (2), WI 92/93 (4), NZ 92/93 (3), Eng 94 (6), NZ 93/94 (3), SA 93/94 (3)

Best bowling against each country:			5WI	10WM
England	5-82	Edgbaston 93	1	0
India	1-150	Sydney 91/92	0	0
New Zealand	6-31	Hobart 93/94	1	0
South Africa	7-56	Sydney 93/94	2	1
Sri Lanka	3-11	Colombo 92/93	0	0
West Indies	7-52	Melbourne 92/93	1	0

Coopers & Lybrand world rating (bowling): 4 (877)

WASIM AKRAM

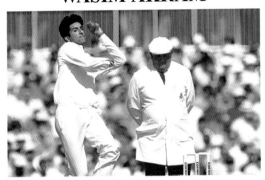

Full name: Wasim Akram
Born: 03/06/66 Lahore, Pakistan
Country: Pakistan
Left-arm fast bowler - Left-hand middle order batsman
Test debut: 25/01/85 v New Zealand-Eden Park, Auckland

Test Career Record: *Batting & Fielding*

MAT	Inns	N/O	Runs	H/S	Avg	100s	50s	Cat
53	69	10	1153	123	19.54	1	4	17

Test Career Record: *Bowling*

Balls	Runs	Wkts	Avg	Best	5WI	10WM	BPW
12014	5203	222	23.43	7-119	15	3	54.11

Overseas tours: Aus 84/85, 86/87, 88/89, 89/90, 91/92, 92/93, NZ 84/85, 88/89, 92/93, 93/94, SL 85/86, Ind 86/87, 89/90, Eng 87, 92, WI 87/88, 92/93, SA 92/93, Zim 92/93, Ban 88/89, Sharjah: 84/85, 85/86, 86/87, 88/89, 89/90, 90/91, 91/92, 92/93, 93/94, WC: Aus & NZ 91/92, Pak under 23: SL 84/85,

Test matches: NZ 84/85 (2), SL 85/86 (3), SL 85/86 (3), WI 86/87 (2), Ind 86/87 (5), Eng 87 (5), Eng (2), WI 87/88 (3), Ind 89/90 (4), Aus 89/90 (3), NZ 90/91 (2), WI 90/91 (3), SL 91/92 (3), Eng 92 (4), NZ 92/93 (1), WI 92/93 (3), Zim 93/94 (2), NZ 93/94 (3)

Best bowling against each country:			5WI	10WM
Australia	6-62	Melbourne 89/90	3	1
England	6-67	Oval 92	2	0
India	5-96	Calcutta 86/87	2	0
New Zealand	7-119	Wellington 93/94	5	2
Sri Lanka	4-55	Colombo 85/86	0	0
West Indies	6-91	Faisalabad 86/87	2	0
Zimbabwe	5-65	Rawalpindi 93/94	1	0

Coopers & Lybrand world rating (bowling): 10= (674)

STEVE WATKIN

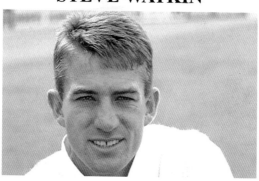

Full name: Steven Llewellyn Watkin
Born: 15/09/64 Duffryn Rhondda, Maesteg, Glamorgan
Country: England
Right-arm fast medium bowler - Right-hand lower order batsman
Test debut: 06/06/91 v West Indies - Headingley, Leeds

Test Career Record: *Batting & Fielding*

MAT	Inns	N/O	Runs	H/S	Avg	100s	50s	Cat
3	5	0	25	13	5.00	0	0	1

Test Career Record: *Bowling*

Balls	Runs	Wkts	Avg	Best	5WI	10WM	BPW
534	305	11	27.72	4-65	0	0	48.54

Overseas tours: WI 93/94, Eng A: Zim 89/90, Pak & SL 90/91, WI 91/92

Test matches: WI 91 (2), Aus 93 (1)

Best bowling against each country:			5WI	10WM
Australia	4-65	The Oval 93	0	0
West Indies	3-38	Headingley 91	0	0

Coopers & Lybrand world rating (bowling): 56 (231)*

WILLIE WATSON

Full name: William Watson
Born: 31/08/65 Auckland, New Zealand
Country: New Zealand
Right-arm fast medium - Right-hand lower order batsman
Test debut: 24/07/86 v England - Lord's, London

Test Career Record: Batting & Fielding								
MAT	Inns	N/O	Runs	H/S	Avg	100s	50s	Cat
15	18	6	60	11	5.00	0	0	4

Test Career Record: Bowling							
Balls	Runs	Wkts	Avg	Best	5WI	10WM	BPW
3486	1387	40	34.67	6-78	1	0	87.15

Overseas tours: SL 85/86, Eng 86, 90, Aus 87/88, 89/90, 90/91, 93/94, Ind 88/89, Pak 90/91, Zim 92/93, Sharjah 85/86, 87/88, WC: Ind 87/88, Young NZ: Zim 88/89

Test matches: Eng 86 (2), Aus 89/90 (1), Pak 90/91 (3), SL 90/91 (3), Eng 91/92 (1), Zim 92/93 (2), Aus 92/93 (2), Aus 93/94 (1)

Best bowling against each country:			5WI	10WM
Australia	3-43	Auckland 92/93	0	0
England	2-41	Auckland 91/92	0	0
Pakistan	6-78	Lahore 90/91	1	0
Sri Lanka	4-121	Wellington 90/91	0	0
Zimbabwe	1-3	Harare 92/93	0	0

Coopers & Lybrand world rating (bowling): 35 (346)*

MARK WAUGH

Full name: Mark Edward Waugh
Born: 02/06/65 Canterbury, Sydney, New South Wales
Country: Australia
Right-hand middle order batsman - Right-arm medium
bowler
Test debut: 25/01/91 v England - Adelaide Oval

Test Career Record: *Batting & Fielding*

MAT	Inns	N/O	Runs	H/S	Avg	100s	50s	Cat
33	52	3	1944	139*	39.67	5	12	46

Test Career Record: *Bowling*

Balls	Runs	Wkts	Avg	Best	5WI	10WM	BPW
1740	788	23	34.26	4-80	0	0	75.65

Overseas tours: WI 90/91, SL 92/93, NZ 92/93, Eng 93,
WC: NZ 91/92

Test matches: Eng 90/91 (2), WI 90/91 (5), Ind 91/92
(4), SL 92/93 (3), WI 92/93 (5), NZ 92/93 (2), Eng 93 (6),
NZ 93/94 (3), SA 93/94 (3)

Highest score against each country:			100s	50s
England	138	Adelaide 90/91	2	5
India	34	Melbourne 91/92	0	0
New Zealand	111	Hobart 93/94	1	1
South Africa	84	Melbourne 93/94	0	1
Sri Lanka	56	Colombo 92/93	0	1
West Indies	139*	St John's 90/91	2	4

Coopers & Lybrand world rating (batting): 26 (568)